"If you're looking for a compan[ion] and to help you apply ancient Scripture to your modern-day life, look no further! *God Values Our Daily Steps* offers a daily short synopsis which brings the word to life in an easily understandable and compelling way, moving us from Bible reading to Bible living. This book is the perfect partner to your Bible reading plan!"

—ERICA WIGGENHORN, award-winning author of *An Unexpected Revival: Experiencing God's Goodness through Disappointment and Doubt*

"*God Values Our Daily Steps* challenges us to go back to our first love as believers and embrace the truth that only God is worthy of our devotion and love. The world is constantly changing, but God's word is anchored in the unchanged character of a holy and faithful God. This book will take us back to our spiritual roots grounded in our relationship with Jesus Christ."

—GERALD LONG, former regional director, Fellowship of Christian Athletics

"*God Values Our Daily Steps* is an incredible tool for every Christian. Along with key highlights from the book of Genesis, this book provides practical applications you can use immediately. Carl Barrett's straight talk makes God's word understandable, relatable, and applicable to our lives today. This series has life-changing potential. I'll be keeping this book on my shelf for years to come!"

—KIM ERICKSON, author of *Predicting Jesus: A 6-Week Study of the Messianic Prophecies in Isaiah*

"This devotional guide is an overflow of Carl Barrett's heart for God and his dedication to years of mentoring and discipling others into a daily walk with our heavenly Father. The daily studies are sure to deepen your walk with God and develop your heart to know God better."

—KEITH WHEELER, chief sales officer, Flowers Foods

"Carl Barrett is one of the most genuine and passionate people I have enjoyed the privilege of being acquainted with in my life. This book is written from the heart and reveals his desire to see people better know Jesus as their Lord and Savior."

—MIKE MCCONATHY, retired men's basketball coach, Northwestern State University

God Values Our Daily Steps

About the Series

Monday Blues to Sunday Pews is a grassroots series of Christian books that will lead us on a journey through each book of the Bible, one step at a time. They will cover key verses and topics within each chapter that were life-changing then and are still life-changing today. They will inspire and encourage the "intentional" believer to move from a rut of complacency to a life that brings value to the Lord by how they live. This journey, will broaden and deepen our knowledge of God's expectations for each of us. We will learn the importance of obtaining the message from God's word and sustaining it daily through real-life application!

At the end of each chapter, as you pick up some missing nuggets in your life, you will have the opportunity to plant and share those nuggets that impacted you on our website—www.mondaybluestosundaypews.com. They will be stored like a journal and used as a testimony for others, and maybe as a reminder for you in the future. But most importantly, Monday Blues to Sunday Pews will donate over half of our proceeds to support the mission field, help the needy, and assist organizations in distributing God's word, globally. Remember this passage in Matt 16:24: *We're called to be intentional followers of Jesus Christ—daily!*

- Monday—Meditate on one Scripture in an area where you need help to refresh your mindset.

- Tuesday—Tell someone about your daily journey as you begin. Someone needs to hear it, too!

- Wednesday—Walk with a close friend and share your experience, as you're walking with God!

- Thursday—Thankful for one thing that happened this week. Showing gratitude is a huge step.

- Friday—Focus on another area in your life that needs improvement; we all have them.

- Saturday—Share one significant impact from the week with someone who also needs uplifting.

- Sunday—Serve in some capacity in your church or community—connect, serve, and grow.

God Values Our Daily Steps

A Fifty-Day Devotional Guide through Genesis

CARL BARRETT

Monday Blues to Sunday Pews

RESOURCE *Publications* · Eugene, Oregon

GOD VALUES OUR DAILY STEPS
A Fifty-Day Devotional Guide through Genesis

Monday Blues to Sunday Pews

Copyright © 2022 Carl Barrett. All rights reserved. Except for brief quotations in critical publications or reviews, no part of this book may be reproduced in any manner without prior written permission from the publisher. Write: Permissions, Wipf and Stock Publishers, 199 W. 8th Ave., Suite 3, Eugene, OR 97401.

Resource Publications
An Imprint of Wipf and Stock Publishers
199 W. 8th Ave., Suite 3
Eugene, OR 97401

www.wipfandstock.com

PAPERBACK ISBN: 978-1-6667-5191-8
HARDCOVER ISBN: 978-1-6667-5192-5
EBOOK ISBN: 978-1-6667-5193-2

11/17/22

Scripture quotations are taken from the Holy Bible, New Living Translation, copyright © 1996, 2004, 2015 by Tyndale House Foundation. Used by permission of Tyndale House Publishers, Inc., Carol Stream, Illinois 60188. All rights reserved.

Contents

Acknowledgments — xi
About the Author — xiii
Preface — xv
Introduction — xix

WEEK 1 | We're Created for *Much More*! — 1
Chapter 1: Godly Imitator — 3
Chapter 2: United with God — 5
Chapter 3: The Enemy Attacks — 8
Chapter 4: How We Respond — 11
Chapter 5: Be Accountable — 13

WEEK 2 | A Blessing to Know & Grow — 17
Chapter 6: Aim for God — 19
Chapter 7: His Presence — 22
Chapter 8: Pleasing to God — 24
Chapter 9: He Promises — 26
Chapter 10: Don't Rebel — 28

WEEK 3 | His Covenant—Our Commitment — 31
Chapter 11: Godly Accomplisher — 33
Chapter 12: All In — 35
Chapter 13: Right Perspective — 37
Chapter 14: Our Helper — 40
Chapter 15: Transparent with God — 42

WEEK 4 | SEEK & FIND … 45

Chapter 16: Seek His Counsel … 47
Chapter 17: Inward Change … 49
Chapter 18: God Knows … 51
Chapter 19: Desires Can Kill … 53
Chapter 20: The Way Out … 56

WEEK 5 | His Goodness Prevails … 59

Chapter 21: Rest Assured … 61
Chapter 22: Developing Us … 63
Chapter 23: His Good Season … 66
Chapter 24: The Little Things … 68
Chapter 25: God's Ways … 70

WEEK 6 | Godly Path … 73

Chapter 26: Our Opportunity … 75
Chapter 27: Genuine Honesty … 77
Chapter 28: God's Clarity … 79
Chapter 29: Diligent Endurance … 81
Chapter 30: Wait! … 83

WEEK 7 | Chosen to Glorify … 85

Chapter 31: Don't Compare … 87
Chapter 32: Diligently Prepare … 89
Chapter 33: A Past Made Right … 91
Chapter 34: God Sees All … 93
Chapter 35: Set Apart … 95

WEEK 8 | The Big Picture … 97

Chapter 36: Godly Evidence … 99
Chapter 37: Our Role … 101
Chapter 38: He's Fair & Faithful … 103
Chapter 39: Don't Compromise … 105
Chapter 40: God's Timing … 107

WEEK 9 | Building Godly Character — 109

Chapter 41: His Appointed Gifts — 111
Chapter 42: Spirit Trumps Flesh — 113
Chapter 43: Faith Trumps Fear — 116
Chapter 44: Overcome Suffering — 118
Chapter 45: Real Love — 121

WEEK 10 | Blessed Relations — 125

Chapter 46: Know His Sovereignty — 127
Chapter 47: Coming Together — 130
Chapter 48: Perfect Father — 133
Chapter 49: Instructions for His Appointed — 135
Chapter 50: Good Trumps Evil — 138

Glossary — 141
Bibliography — 175

Acknowledgments

Writing a book doesn't just take drive, time, discipline, and diligence, but it takes motivation and inspiration. And I have so many people to thank who pushed me not only to write this book but also to submit it to publishers. From friends back home in East Texas, to my wife and son (Sheila and Brian). But also, many family members and several brothers and sisters in Christ who inspired and motivated me to press on.

I wish to personally thank the following people for their contributions, inspiration, knowledge, and help in creating this book: Thank you to the following individuals—without their support, this book would not have been written: Kenny Pope, Ray Pirolo, Kim Erickson, Erica Wiggenhorn, B. J. Garrett, and Steve Dillard. There are also so many friends and acquaintances globally on Facebook that really encouraged me. And thanks to the Wipf and Stock Publishers family for taking a chance on me, friends at Radical Ministry for their unbelievable words of motivation, American Bible Society for words of encouragement, Prison Fellowship Ministries for their support, and Blackaby Ministries International for their words of inspiration.

About the Author

Carl Barrett is a retired professional in the food industry for one of the largest commercial bakers in the country. He held various management positions for almost forty years, where he had the opportunity to work with some of the largest retailers in the world.

But to honestly know Carl is to see his work in the church, community, missions, and prisons throughout his life. Because there lies his passion for helping people to better themselves by following Christ as their daily example. He's always aspired to help others understand how God's word can be applied and impact our everyday life. And not just individually but on others around us.

He's served as a personal development mentor for the Texas Juvenile Justice Department and Prison Fellowship Ministry in state penitentiaries, juvenile detention, and detention centers across multiple states. He's also served as a teacher and preacher in various prisons and was an instructor for National Fatherhood Initiatives. He has taught Sunday School in multiple churches from the range of two years of age to ninety-two years of age. He's led hospitality and first impressions ministry teams at numerous churches. And he's currently a volunteer for CASA (Court Appointed Special Advocate) and helps the ministry team at Under the Bridge Church for homeless people in Tyler, Texas.

He holds a BSBA from Madison University and studied biblical and theological studies at Texas Baptist Institute. In addition, he's attended many seminars and certified programs at some of the largest institutions in the United States in the areas of human relations development, motivational leadership, and the empowerment of engagement. He's also written a self-help business book entitled *Searching for Your Comfort Zone*.

Preface

The vital signs are profound and compelling. In 2018, Pew Research Center conducted a poll where many Christians were asked this question: "Why do you go to church?" Over 80 percent said, *"To get closer to God."* But in an "alarming" report released by the American Bible Society in 2020, *only 9 percent of Christians read God's word daily.*[1]

Equally troubling, in another poll conducted by Barna Group in 2020, people were asked if America would be worse off, the same, or better without the Bible; only 49 percent said it would be worse, 39 percent said it would be the same, and 13 percent said it would be better—what a disparity!

Participants were also asked if they agreed with this statement, *"The Bible contains everything a person needs to know to live a meaningful life." Only 37 percent agreed strongly, 31 percent agreed somewhat, and 32 percent disagreed with the statement.*[2]

These staggering statistics reveal a stark contrast between *man's expectations of God's word* versus *God's expectations of man understanding his word.* Is man's perception of the word clouded by too much worldliness (Rom 12:2)?[3]

If we look at the turmoil and confusion in this country and the world today—there's an obvious telltale sign our daily steps with God's word are not in order—we are way out of line!

So, I beg the question. Are we, as intentional believers in Jesus Christ, "actually" growing? Because based on these stats above, something is missing. But what could be the underlying cause?

Are we sustaining the teachings from God's word on Sunday throughout the week? Are we applying his word to every part of our life? And here's

---

1. Pew Research Center, "Top Reasons US Adults Give," para. 1.
2. Clark, "2020 'State of the Bible,'" paras. 2, 3.
3. The NLT version of Scripture is used throughout this book.

the critical question: "Do we truly understand the importance of being in step with our Lord every day?"

I love this powerful statement from Dr. Tony Evans on spiritual growth. "When you discover He's all you have, you will discover He's all you need!"[4] *With that said—believers should know this—God must be present in every step of our daily life.*

If God is a stranger to us, we are less likely to believe his word and find actual value in his message. The only cure is to spend more time in God's word, observing its message—interpreting its meaning—and applying it in our lives. Putting this into action gives us that connection with our Almighty God and his power at use in our daily lives. And trust me—it's then when we will see the value of our relationship with him!

This book aims to identify a problem in many today: moving from a rut of spiritual complacency to absolute dependency upon the word of God "in all areas of our life" (Phil 4:9). We have a power source of wisdom, truth, and understanding that we can tap into daily (Heb 4:12-13). *But do we use it to its capacity?* (Col 3:16)

A heart-pounding diagnosis is this—believers are either *active and intentional* in their daily steps with the Lord or *inactive and unintentional—and going nowhere! So which area do you fall into?*

Here are the facts; *our actions intentional or unintentional hinge on this—the condition of our heart.* Because the heart is the driving force behind our motives and desires. Wherever your treasure is, there the desires of your heart will also be (Matt 6:21). *And Jesus even reminds us in Matthew 13, in the Parable of the Sower, that the seed is the word of God, and when it was scattered amongst four soils, how it produces is based on the condition of that person's heart.*

Galatians 5:25 reminds us that if we live by the Spirit, we will be in step with the Spirit. This powerful passage shows us that when we take steps with God, we feel his closeness, direction, and help in times of need. Then we feel his comfort, peace, *and that understanding of what is right and wrong in our lives* (2 Tim 3:16-17). We know and feel the impact of our spiritual walk because it illustrates our "Christlike" behavior and what's truly important to us, but also God. These steps demonstrate our actual value in the One who created us. God treasures our efforts and time with him because they glorify his name.

Every day we need to remind ourselves when we are out of step with God, we're not in line with a purpose and plan that will be for our good! So, the red flags should be significant when something or someone redirects

---

4 Sermon Notes by Dr. Tony Evans, "Maturity," 0:24-0:30.

our steps! Because that's when the Holy Spirit is convicting and counseling us—trying to lead us back to the right course in our lives.

So, if you feel like your heart, soul, and mind needs to be renewed, refreshed, restored, and reinvigorated—God's word is your source, and the benefits will be rewarding. And here's the power punch when God's word goes out: *"It is the same with my word. I send it out, and it always produces fruit. It will accomplish all I want it to, and it will prosper everywhere I send it"* (Isa 55:11).

It will prosper if we put it into action, but we must be intentional in our daily steps with the Lord! Today we don't need pew warmers; we need pew doers (putting it into action)!

Introduction

> You, dear children, are from God and have overcome them because the One who is in you is greater than the one who is in the world. (1 John 4:4)

Remember the funny movie *What About Bob*? It was about a man entirely debilitated by his fears, anxieties, and worries about today's world. Doctor Leo Marvin had a powerful line in the movie: "The greatest psychiatrist in the world is the one right inside of you." He wrote a book and recommended it as a daily tool in Bob's life: *Baby Steps: A Guide to Living Life One Step at a Time*.

Such a cliché, but for believers, we have the Greatest Authority living within us today and the Greatest Guide of all—God's word! We all start on ground level; the peaks and valleys in life that we choose are up to us! *Our daily achievements and time with the Lord should be a step UP from yesterday because when we're striving for his presence, we will realize our efforts did make a difference!*

When I wrote a self-help business book twenty years ago entitled *Searching for Your Comfort Zone*, I used my experience to show the readers how to "Establish a Solid Relationship with the Customer." The main message was to illustrate how to connect with the right people in the right place at the right time, which could elevate their career paths. The critical components of the book were built on the foundation of trust, commitment, dependability, accountability, and integrity.

And this book, *God Values our Daily Steps*, has the exact parallels in how to attain that connection with God daily. Suppose we establish a solid relationship with our Lord based on the five critical components listed above. In that case, it will elevate our closeness with him: By trusting in his word, committing our all to him, depending on him more than ourselves, and being accountable believers. God wants to reveal himself to us in mighty ways through a growing relationship—that is accomplished through the power of his word and Spirit! Sometimes we simply need to start anew, from the beginning, and there's no better place to start than in Genesis, *taking those invaluable beginning steps with God!*

A journey through the book of Genesis is a significant starting point for all of us. It shows the beginning steps of God's creation, his nature, his inspired revelation, and the importance of us knowing the actual characteristics of our Creator and Heavenly Father. It will reveal who we are as his devoted followers, which should be a light in this dark world.

Why Genesis? Because it probably has the most to say about the problems we're seeing in this world today. From the sanctity of life—to our struggles with sin—choices in life—to life and death. From the beginning, God created you and me for a purpose that would fit into his excellent plan. Since he took pleasure in creating us, he wants that authentic, genuine, and growing relationship! He wants to see "our real purpose" in life come to fruition—one with a heart committed to him and who illustrates a genuine love for the One Who deserves all our time and attention.

Remember, our God is a jealous God (Exod 34:14). God is rightly jealous when worship, praise, honor, or adoration is given to idols or others—*when it belongs to him alone!*

Each day with our Lord is so precious! It's those quiet quality times where we can relate with relevance—reset our minds, defocus from the negatives—and focus on him! (Col 3:2; Phil 4:8).

As you take this journey, ingrain this in your mind: *"a daily process should always lead to progress!"* Second Peter 1 reminds us that "we're given every resource for living a Godly life"; in other words, there's no excuse and no scapegoat. *If we're genuine and loving students of his word, we will not find it difficult to cling to the Christian values he's prescribed for you and me.*

Will there be barriers? Yes! The enemy wants to remove any prescriptive plan in our life that brings honor to Jesus Christ. While God wants us to glorify him—the enemy detests anything that brings honor to the Lord. The enemy will do everything in his power to keep us from walking with the Lord, because he does not want us to reflect anything Christlike in our daily life. He will put up all the barriers and distractions because he wants us to be stuck in a stagnate life—going nowhere. Remember this; *when we're on fire for the Lord, the enemy wants to put our fire out!* When we're yearning, yielding, and growing, the enemy will intensify his weapons of spiritual warfare. *But* that's where fervent *prayer and God's word* will be your power source! Put on the "whole" armor of God and get into the battle (Eph 6:11)! *You must be all in for the Lord—every day!*

In my almost ten years of service in the prison ministry as a mentor and chaplain, I bonded with inmates from maximum security to detention centers to juvenile detention. We established a unity of respect, trust, and accountability; there was no room for hypocrisy or phoniness. We knew each other like family; our worship and fellowship went to unimaginable heights. Brothers would open up in areas of their life that the enemy wanted them to bottle up and never discuss. Prison officials were impacted by witnessing the power of the Holy Spirit at work!

We bonded and grew when we completely surrendered our all to God in obedience. We witnessed powerful testimonies of restoration, reconciliation, forgiveness, and love that only God could produce. Over time they came up with a tagline; this *would be our battle cry—our action words of accountability*: "You're either all in . . . or you're not in at all!" Many of them would make all types of excuses—so it came down to this: *"All believers must instill in the fabric of their being a wholehearted submission to His word and all that it can "provide and produce."*

In this journey, *we will either be proactive or procrastinate* because it will hinge on the intentions of our hearts! Our spiritual approach and application will be imperative in preparing ourselves daily to connect with God because this fifty-day guide requires individual responsibility and dedication. It will demonstrate our "real" testimony of obedience and commitment to his word. So, before the journey begins, here's the key question: *"Do you want to accelerate & elevate your daily steps with the Lord—feel his closeness and make a difference today?"*

Psalm 1 (NLT) says, "Oh, the joys of those who do not follow the advice of the wicked, stand around with sinners, or join in with mockers. But they delight in the law of the Lord, meditating on it day and night. They are like trees planted along the riverbank, bearing fruit each season. Their leaves never wither, and they prosper in all they do."

Always remember, when the enemy is on the attack, acknowledge your weak and most vulnerable areas and go to God's words that apply to those areas. Memorize the scriptures to your advantage and say them aloud. That's precisely what Christ did in the wilderness against the enemy. He countered the enemy with the word of God. It works when it's used to its powerful benefit!

When your roots are planted, grounded, nurtured, growing, and spreading, that life-changing experience and transformation are happening. That second, when you realize what you have inside, it's only a matter of time. *A good seed always rises to mass production, while a bad seed is barren.* He will provide—if you want to produce! And it starts with you and me—*now*!

WEEK 1

We're Created for *Much More*!

Gen 1–5

In week 1, we'll see in the first five chapters the pleasure and delight God took in creating everything—especially humankind. But then, we will see a significant shift from God's pleasure to his displeasure because of man's wicked and defiant ways. In God's eyes, the creation of humans was astonishing, excellent, and marvelous—for we were wonderfully and fearfully made, as God's word reminds us in Ps 139. All that God had created from the beginning was good, but one wrong choice led to an unsuitable state. In these chapters, we will see life-changing experiences we can even apply in our lives today.

God's Creation fascinates everyone because people are searching for answers and a clear understanding of God's Sovereignty and his resolve. Maybe that's why Gen 1 is probably the most-read chapter in the Bible. From the beginning of time, God's word tells us that the Creator shaped our lives. He formed us in his image, breathed life into us, gave man a companion, and provided guidelines for us to live by each day. Nothing has ever been written and recorded with so much truth.

As we prepare to start this journey in Genesis, there's a slogan we could all apply and live by each day, *"United We Stand, Divided We Fall." Suppose we would all inspire unity and bind ourselves under the authority of God, working in unison with his plan. In that case, it will not likely doom us to fail in this life's journey.*

CHAPTER 1

Godly Imitator

> Then God said, "Let us make human beings in our image, to be like us. They will reign over the fish in the sea, the birds in the sky, the livestock, all the wild animals on the earth, and the small animals that scurry along the ground." So, God created human beings in his own image. In the image of God, he created them; male and female he created them. Then God blessed them and said, "Be fruitful and multiply. Fill the earth and govern it. Reign over the fish in the sea, the birds in the sky, and all the animals that scurry along the ground." Then God said, "Look! I have given you every seed-bearing plant throughout the earth and all the fruit trees for your food. And I have given every green plant as food for all the wild animals, the birds in the sky, and the small animals that scurry along the ground—everything that has life." And that is what happened. Then God looked over all he had made, and he saw that it was very good! And evening passed and morning came, marking the sixth day." (Gen 1:26–31)

In all his divine ways from the beginning of time, God clearly shows us how we got here, Who we came from, why we're here, our "real" purpose in life, the Truth of his word, and the cause of all our problems. He reveals to us *his path* of "life and death."

By breathing his breath of life into man, he created the man and woman "in his own image" (Gen 1:27). I love the New Living Translation of Gen 1:26 for it tells us, "Let us make human beings *in our image, to be more like Us*." The power of this passage is the work of the Father, Son, and Holy Spirit in our lives, because as believers, we should glorify God in all that we do as his children, magnifying Jesus Christ as his faithful followers, and honoring the Holy Spirit because his work in us reveals Christ, our King!

We have an eternal spirit, just as God has. We can reason, choose good or evil, and love; we have emotions and intellect like our Heavenly Father. We are intricately (very detailed) created by the Almighty One! We're reflections of God's image, so we should take honor in knowing *that he made us as his own. He stamped his approval on all of creation, and most importantly, you and me—so we should never downplay who we are, because as believers, our identity is in Christ alone!* As John MacArthur once said, "No adjective goes in front of the title name Christians. He stands alone as our real identification in this world!"[1]

He chose us before the beginning of the earth's foundation (Eph 1:4). And make no mistake about it—in God's eyes, he's placed a value and worth on you and me, because we are his own possession, and we have an inheritance. And to show us how important we are—he paid the ultimate price on that cross through Christ his Son—our Savior! *He invested in us—and as God's chosen ones, it should be our goal and intent to attain his return on that investment!*

You and I share many of God's characteristics: love, patience, forgiveness, kindness, and faithfulness, *but how we handle those Godly characteristics in our daily life is key to his name being glorified.* Once he stamped his approval on you and me, *his expectations for us have risen to a higher level.*

In this powerful statement by Paul in 1 Cor 11:1, "And you should imitate me, just as I imitate Christ." He's telling the Corinthians to follow him because he follows Christ. The Corinthians didn't know much about the life of Christ, so Paul knew the best way to point them to his Lord was to show them someone whom they trusted that best represented and imitated Jesus Christ. And not out of arrogance or stating he was sinless and perfect, but to show the closest example of a Christlike follower, he said "Look at me!" *Can the world say that about us as Christians today?*

> And whatever you do or say, do it as a representative of the Lord Jesus, giving thanks through him to God the Father. (Col 3:17)

---

1. This quote came from a sermon by MacArthur that I attended.

CHAPTER 2

United with God

> Then the Lord God said, "It is not good for the man to be alone. I will make a helper who is just right for him." . . . So the Lord God caused the man to fall into a deep sleep. While the man slept, the Lord God took out one of the man's ribs and closed up the opening. Then the Lord God made a woman from the rib, and he brought her to the man. (Gen 2:18, 21–22)

A powerful passage is when God says, "It's not good for man to be alone." God did not complete the job until Adam had a female counterpart." This passage is pivotal and significant in Gen 2, for it lays the foundation of unity throughout the word of God!

To ensure the work was good and completed, God would create a helper for Adam, which would fulfill God's intention for humanity—because one man couldn't do it alone. Adam would need to understand the importance of a female helper—because, without her, God's entire design for the function of humanity would fail.

There was absolute and complete joy when Adam and Eve were together with God in the garden! They were happy and satisfied because they walked and talked with God. He was their friend—he was the nucleus of their relationship. God's word reminds us in Mic 6:8 that he created us for fellowship with him—and he desires for us to walk humbly with him.

So, if God is the central point and at the heart of a marriage today, there will also be joy. Without God in the heart of a man and wife's relationship they will lack Christlike love, faithfulness, peace, unity, joy, and harmony. We must understand the importance of having God in our marriage as he initially created. If not, then we're apart from his will—and we're not united in his plan. Remember this statement—*when we revolve our lives around Jesus Christ, life's problems are easier to resolve.*

And here's the key—God made us a top priority when he breathed the breath of life into man. So, for us today, it's vitally important that we prioritize God in our marriage, which means knowing our Creator and Father in our hearts and reflecting him in our daily actions. When we do this our Heavenly Father is praised, Christ is exalted, and the Holy Spirit is valued and cherished. If the Lord is our top priority, he's regarded and treated as Someone important in our everyday life.

The psalmist tells us in Ps 27:4, "The one thing I ask of the Lord—the thing I seek most—is to live in the house of the Lord all the days of my life, *delighting in the Lord's perfections* and meditating in his Temple." What a beautiful depiction where we should realize the importance of reaching and sustaining the presence of the Lord in our daily lives and knowing that when we agree with him, we're in step with his perfect purpose and plan. When we're of one mind with our Lord, it keeps us in one accord with all his attributes and teachings. It establishes Christlike peace and joy in our lives, bonded in a state of unity that demonstrates our actual position in Christ.

God's word reminds us in Eph 4 when we're united, we're no longer acting like immature Christians. We won't be tossed and blown around with confusion by other teachings, and we are not easily swayed. Instead, we will speak more in his truth and love growing more and more like Christ; we will be his true children of Light!

Suppose parents disagree when raising and disciplining their children. In that case, there will be confusion and a breakdown in the family system, and the child often goes astray. If a teacher and student disagree on a significant subject, the student will fail in most cases. If an employer and employee disagree with establishing their goals, more than likely, there will be a shortfall. When a pastor and body disagree, more than likely, there will be division and discord. But, more importantly, if we disagree with our Creator, there will be disunity. And that will open the enemy's door to attack and break us down. And when that separation occurs in our life, it's a domino effect that can trickle down to everyone around us.

Paul tells us in Phil 2 that the key to having the same mind as Christ is in our attitude of humility. Christ was God in the flesh, and he still did not cling to his rights as God. Instead, he humbled himself in one accord with his Father because he knew there was a mission to be accomplished. *And that one sole mission continues today in and through us.*

Having the mind of Jesus Christ means we understand God's plan in this world. Luke 19:10 reminds us that the Son of Man came to seek and save what was lost. He plans to restore creation to its original state and splendor—and provide salvation for all through his Son Jesus.

But unfortunately, there's a lot of divisiveness in this country and the world today. Christ's followers are not surprised by this division, because they can discern those spiritual things that the natural man—the unbelieving world cannot understand or see (1 Cor 2:16). But believers in Jesus understand this key factor—the importance of building unity, so more of Christ is revealed for the world to see!

God had a higher calling when he brought man and woman together, one in the flesh serving Christ—because as believers every Christian has a calling on their life. We were designed before the foundation of the world to be his workmanship, glorifying him as we bring forth the fruit that he desires in our daily life (Eph 1:4–5).

We discover that "calling" by walking closely with him, pursuing and applying obedience in our life, and offering ourselves as living sacrifices (Rom 12:1–2). As we develop that keen sensitivity to his voice, *we move forward as one*! Why? Because we're united with him—and less likely to be divisive.

> I appeal to you, dear brothers and sisters, by the authority of our Lord Jesus Christ, to live in harmony with each other. Let there be no divisions in the church. Rather, be of one mind, united in thought and purpose. (1 Cor 1:10)

CHAPTER 3

The Enemy Attacks

> The serpent was the shrewdest of all the wild animals the Lord God had made. One day he asked the woman, "Did God really say you must not eat the fruit from any of the trees in the garden?" "Of course, we may eat fruit from the trees in the garden," the woman replied. "It's only the fruit from the tree in the middle of the garden that we are not allowed to eat. God said, 'You must not eat it or even touch it; if you do, you will die.'" "You won't die!" the serpent replied to the woman. "God knows that your eyes will be opened as soon as you eat it, and you will be like God, knowing both good and evil." The woman was convinced. She saw that the tree was beautiful, and its fruit looked delicious, and she wanted the wisdom it would give her. So, she took some of the fruit and ate it. Then she gave some to her husband, who was with her, and he ate it, too. At that moment their eyes were opened, and they suddenly felt shame at their nakedness. So, they sewed fig leaves together to cover themselves. (Gen 3:1–7)

God provided Adam and Eve with a life of perfection—one they could enjoy with many wonderful blessings. But first, they had to follow one command: "*Do not* eat from the tree God had forbidden. "

But the enemy is on the prowl and out to deceive with his sly and shrewd choice of words. *He is so suave in his deceptive ways that he can trick anyone into not believing in God's goodness.* For example, Eve tells Satan they *could eat from any tree(s) in the garden*, just not the one God forbade. But this is how cunning Satan is: *he took Eve's mind off all the good trees and God's goodness* and twisted her focus on the one tree God forbid (the tree of the knowledge of good and evil). God told them there would be consequences if they ate from this tree, *but the enemy told Eve entirely the opposite of what God said, and she fell for it! The enemy minimized the penalty by telling her that they would not die.* And after experiencing such peace and joy with their Creator, they fell for Satan's deceiving words. Did they truly understand the consequences of their disobedience? When we disobey, do we genuinely understand the result of our sins?

All along, Adam and Eve could eat from any tree in the Garden, except for the one—the tree of the knowledge of good and evil. And that one wrong choice—when they had so many good trees to choose from led to disaster. Even for us today one choice that's not in line with God's plan can easily separate us from the will of God and lead us down a spiraling path of destruction. The only way to counter the enemy's tactics is by attaining God's knowledge through his word and heeding direction from the Holy Spirit. We cannot achieve his knowledge by taking shortcuts in life, such as in the case of Adam and Eve when they fell for Satan's lie. Because *knowledge and understanding come from the Lord's mouth* (Prov 2:6).

God's word reminds us that the serpent is the "shrewdest" of all the wild animals. In man's definition of shrewd, it has both a good and bad connotation. The good is clever and prudent in finding hidden possibilities or devising new strategies to get a difficult or challenging task done, and the bad is obvious.

So, *here's how shrewd the enemy works. He can take something meant for our good, distort it, and make it look bad and lead us to believe we don't need it. And on the flip side, the enemy can take something bad for us and lead us to believe it's good and we need it! And that one choice can lead to our spiritual demise.* He's that cunning!

Yes, we see the deception, temptation, and disobedience in these verses but let's not overlook the pleasures of life that God provided for Adam and Eve. Simply put—they were not content with God's provisions and neglected his goodness. I can only imagine what would have been the outcome *if they had nurtured that wonderful relationship with God and obeyed his command.* And I can only imagine what if they never allowed that one open conversation with the enemy, which opened the door to his deception and led to one destructive choice. If they had been more in tune with God, they would not have lost focus and been easily swayed by the enemy and had an open ear to his deceptive ways. Always remember, God is not opposed to happiness and pleasure, *but he is opposed to anything that takes place over him.*

In our fast-paced life, there will be times when we're called to decline the joys of this world and invest in the greater pleasures of building God's glorious kingdom. But know this: *we will not be disappointed! "For those who seek Him and His righteousness, God has "eternal pleasures" in store"* (Ps 16:11).

So, what secret nugget do we need, which will make it easy for us to decline the things of this world and live out a more intentional focus on God in our daily life? *It's the power of contentment*! When we're satisfied and pleased with the life we contain internally, we know nothing else can take the place of a gratified life of peace and happiness that we possess in him. *We're full, we need no more; it is well with our souls!*

Paul reminds us in Phil 4:11, "Not that I was ever in need, for I have learned how to be content with whatever I have." Paul knew had to be content whether if he had much or little because his power source of contentment came from above! The key to this passage is that Paul was drawing power from his only source—the power of Christ. Paul knew his true purpose in life was being content in his service for the Lord and glorifying him—nothing else mattered.

Christlike contentment comes when we discover our true intentional purpose in life! As his children, we should have that sense of what it is, and we must pursue it! So, we need to stop reaching for our own ideas that please us alone, which can lead to a life of discontentment. But remember, when we strive for areas that honor the Lord, the enemy is waiting to attack. So, stand firm—*refuse to change your position in Christ when the enemy applies pressure from all areas of your life!*

We must live an intentional and content life in the Lord and be steadfast in our faith—and never waver from all that we possess in him. When we expose our weak patterns of life, that will lend the enemy and his demons a position of attack in our most vulnerable areas. Contrary to Adam and Eve, nurture that daily relationship with the Lord and draw close to him. James reminds us in his epistle in 4:7-8, "*So, humble yourselves before God. Resist the devil, and he will flee from you. Come close to God, and God will come close to you. Wash your hands, you sinners; purify your hearts, for your loyalty, is divided between God and the world.*" Recognize that God is our source for all things.

> Stay alert! Watch out for your great enemy, the devil. He prowls around like a roaring lion, looking for someone to devour. Stand firm against him, and be strong in your faith. (1 Pet 5:8-9)

CHAPTER 4

How We Respond

When it was time for the harvest, Cain presented some of his crops as a gift to the Lord. Abel also brought a gift—the best portions of the firstborn lambs from his flock. The Lord accepted Abel and his gift, but he did not accept Cain and his gift. This made Cain very angry, and he looked dejected. "Why are you so angry?" the Lord asked Cain. "Why do you look so dejected? You will be accepted if you do what is right. But if you refuse to do what is right, then watch out! Sin is crouching at the door, eager to control you. But you must subdue it and be its master." (Gen 4:3–7)

These powerful verses pertain to the quality of a Godly heart that possesses unconditional love, care, kindness, gratitude, selflessness, genuine compassion, cooperation, and acceptance. In this passage, it is evident that the quality of Cain's heart did not measure up to God's expectations, *because in Cain's mind, he felt that offering a portion would suffice*—his attitude and motives did not align with God's standards (ouch). While Cain presented to the Almighty Creator "some of his crops," Abel brought forth his "*best*" portion of the "firstborn lambs." So, it was clear that Abel's heart was in line with God's standards. In this illustration, we see a significant contrast between a person with pure motives and another with impure motives.

The power punch is towards the end of these verses, where God tells Cain, *"You will be accepted if you do what is right, but if you refuse to do what is right, then watch out! Sin is crouching at the door and eager to control you. But you must subdue it and be its master."*

Cain was allowed to subdue the sin, waiting to attack and destroy him. All he had to do was give up his jealous anger so that sin would not find a footstool in his life. *Simply put, his heart was not in the right place because he did not respond to God in a manner that was pleasing to him. Instead he reacted out of anger*, which would lead to murder!

Even today, God allows us to make choices that are right in his sight—those that will meet his standards and expectations, which are for our good. *Who would not want to choose and subdue the sins that keep them from the will of God? Who would not want to respond with a pure and intentional heart for the glory of our Lord?*

What is our reaction or response when we do something wrong and someone approaches us? Do we react defensively with destructive emotions? Or do we "respond" with a thoughtful, compassionate, and remorseful heart—one with good intentions to make it right?

Once again, we must remind ourselves that the enemy's goal is to divide and destroy. So, as God's children, we need to counter this tactic by mastering our sin—with the help of the Holy Spirit. We must ground ourselves in the Truth of his word and turn to God and other believers who can encourage and strengthen us.

In this lifelong battle, we must be united with the right motives and attitude that line up with God's word, his will, and his plan! With so much tension around us today, it's vital we *respond—more so than react*.

So often, when we hastily react out of our emotions, it can lead to an aggressive behavior that will ignite disagreements. And in the end, we're spiritually weakened. But when we "take time" to respond (in most cases), we've thought it through, prayed, and sought Godly counsel. Then we're calm, relaxed, and composed in our behavior, and that empowerment comes from the Holy Spirit, a powerful and wonderful feeling when we yield to him and heed his guidance! Portraying and conveying Christlikeness in any circumstance is always rewarding!

> The human heart is the most deceitful of all things, and desperately wicked. Who really knows how bad it is? But I, the Lord, search all hearts and examine secret motives. I give all people their due rewards, according to what their actions deserve. (Jer 17:9–10)

CHAPTER 5

Be Accountable

> This is the written account of the descendants of Adam. When God created human beings, *he made them to be like himself.* He created them male and female, and he blessed them and called them "human." (Gen 5:1–2)

We must spend time understanding all the genealogies in God's word. Why? Because they provide us with absolute solidity, validity, and credibility in the Truth of his word. These records bring the Bible to life and are relatable to people today. They corroborate the facts based on all the studies and research conducted by humanity over the course of history.

In the beginning, genealogies helped God's people remember stories about their lineage because they were recorded and passed down from family to family and from generation to generation. Why? They preserved family traditions and memories because tradition was a big part of their life.

But another key point is that God wanted his children to remember all he had done for them throughout their lives. And even today—he reminds us through the Truth of his word and by his Spirit that he's by our side, and he will never leave us nor forsake us. Because he's our Refuge and Strength—an ever-present need in times of trouble (Ps 46:1–3).

God uses the illustration of genealogies so we can strengthen our faith in the Creator. He even commands us in Deut 6:4–9, to impress these beliefs on our children—to talk about them at home—all the time, day and night! When we pass down to each generation his wonderful work in our lives—it keeps the word alive, powerful, and fresh for his children to remember and continue to pass on.

But they also point out incredible characteristics of God. They show records of family lines with names and where they came from, which clearly illustrates that we are essential to our Heavenly Father as individuals. He loves and values us as his own, demonstrating his importance on the value of family. But the most profound point was to confirm God's promises, and the accuracy of his word, and most notably, the prophecy of our Messiah and Savior, Jesus Christ. Because through Christ, all believers are reconciled to our Heavenly Father as one.

Throughout history and time, we are all related to Adam and Eve, which means that in God's eyes, we're all equal! *Not one of us is better than the other.* We should never forget this when prejudice or hatred enters our minds and hearts; in Christ, we're one! We're all valuable and uniquely created by God. And as his own, that is our common ground on how we can connect with a hurting world that needs healing. So, the next time you're looking for that outreach to someone who is lost in this dark world, as one in Christ, it should open the door of communication so we can share the good news. With the hope they will also believe and be a part of God's family through Christ!

> All praise to God, the Father of our Lord Jesus Christ, who has blessed us with every spiritual blessing in the heavenly realms because we are united with Christ. Even before He made the world, God loved us and chose us in Christ to be holy and without fault in His eyes. God decided in advance to adopt us into His own family by bringing us to Himself through Jesus Christ. Our Father wanted to do this, giving Him great pleasure. (Eph 1:3–5)

So many of us take pride in representing our family bloodline—*but representing the Christ line is always more important!* For God to take pleasure in allowing us to join his family through Jesus Christ, his Son, we should be more accountable for all we're endowed with as his servants on this earth. When we truly recognize our state of accountability as His devoted servants, we will understand our clear responsibilities. And that's upholding those words and actions of grace, mercy, and love towards everyone—not just in our personal family tree, but every branch and limb!

As accountable believers, we should aspire to a reputation and legacy of this entitlement, "Faithful Followers of Jesus Christ!" This label is the highest of honors—for then everyone can see the connecting dots in our lives pointing back to the tree of Jesus Christ! And there's no greater words than any appointed and accountable follower of Jesus Christ would want to hear than this- "Well done, thy good and faithful servant" (Matt 25:23).

> For God knew his people in advance, and he chose them to become like his Son, so that his Son would be the firstborn among many brothers and sisters. And having chosen them, he called

them to come to him. And having called them, he gave them right standing with himself. And having given them right standing, he gave them his glory. (Rom 8:29–30)

WEEK 2

A Blessing to Know & Grow

Gen 6–10

In week 2 (chapters 6–10), we again see God's displeasure with humankind. He graciously gave all humans another chance to make things right—even through their defiance and disobedience. God saw that the wickedness of man was great on the earth, and every intention of their hearts was continuous evil, so God wiped out wickedness, including widespread violence. God will start anew so humanity will have a chance to realize the absolute blessing of knowing him intimately and growing with him in maturity.

God will always seek out those who love him and his commands because he wants to bless, guide, and protect them. When we are resting in God's loving grace, we feel his favor in a strong spiritual sense, for we know God is with us. Nothing can happen apart from his good purpose and plan (Rom 8:28). It's also so comforting to see that we have God's ear as we walk through those dark valleys (Ps 34:15). And to know that our struggle to remain faithful while along he is faithful and true is enlightening (2 Tim 2:13).

When we walk with God like he's our closest friend, we begin to see, feel, experience, and appreciate the little blessings he provides daily. It's an honor and blessing to know and grow closer to him because, as his children, that's our state of happiness—our place of absolute comfort and joy, and nothing can replace that.

In this journey with God, we learn more about listening, observing, interpreting and applying his word in our life, ensuring our understanding of growth and maturity. Second Timothy 3:16–17 reminds us, "All Scripture is inspired by God and is useful to teach us what is true and to make us realize what is wrong in our lives. It corrects us when we are wrong and teaches us to do what is right. God uses it to prepare and equip his people to do every good work."

Walking with God requires:

1. A desire (a strong feeling of wanting something—longing for like yearning; Ps 37:4–5; Matt 6:33).
2. A motive (reason for doing it; Prov 16:2; 21:2; Jas 4:3).
3. An intentional heart (Eph 5:15–17; 1 Chr 16:11; Phil 3:14).
4. A devoted heart (love-loyalty; Rom 12:1; Gal 2:20; 2 Chr 7:14; 16:9).
5. A solid commitment (engaged and obligation; Ps 37:4; Prov 16:3; Col 3:23; 2 Tim 4:7).

And what does it lead to? Connection, growth, and a God-filled mind. Walking with God begins and becomes real when we enter an intimate relationship with him through faith in his Son (Heb 10:22). He becomes our heart's greatest desire.

1. Knowing and growing in him more,
2. Hearing and heeding his voice,
3. Sharing our hearts with him, and
4. Seeking to please him becomes our all-consuming focus!

And that's when you're in his sweet spot!

CHAPTER 6

Aim for God

> The Lord observed the extent of human wickedness on the earth, and he saw that everything they thought or imagined was consistently and totally evil. So, the Lord was sorry he had ever made them and put them on the earth. It broke his heart. And the Lord said, "I will wipe this human race I have created from the face of the earth. Yes, and I will destroy every living thing—all the people, the large animals, the small animals that scurry along the ground, and even the birds of the sky. I am sorry I ever made them." But Noah found favor with the Lord. (Gen 6:5–8)

The people's sins grieved the Lord to the point where he was sorry that he ever made them, and would have to destroy them. He was not regretting the creation of humanity; it was the sin that brought about his sorrow, because sin is what separates humans from the will of God! He created mankind to have an ongoing relationship with them, to be united with him—not the opposite. So, he had to start anew.

We don't know how many died from the flood; some researchers have estimated that it was in the millions. The most compelling point is that only eight were saved—Noah's family. After all, Noah found favor with the Lord and because of that one man's popularity with the Lord, he kept his family from perishing.

Noah was a righteous man, the only blameless man living on earth then. He consistently followed God's plan and enjoyed a relationship with him! He thrived (grew and developed) in many ways to please God.

The flooding of the earth was like giving an artist a brand-new canvas with a broad brush to create something brand new. "Therefore, if anyone is in Christ, he is a new creation; old things have passed away; behold, all things have become new" (2 Cor 5:17). And that new life should give us the drive to strive and aim for all things that please our Lord and Savior—daily.

Unfortunately, many Christians are not striving as much today as we should for God's glory. Instead, we all fall short of his standards (Rom 3:23). This does not mean we will reach perfection, but God's word has set the benchmark, and the threshold is clear. The ultimate question is this: "Are we making great efforts to achieve his standards in our spiritual life?" Because it seems many believers are too complacent, pointing fingers, looking for scapegoats, and don't want to be held accountable.

Until we realize that ownership starts with us (just like Noah), we may stay in that old rut of complacency—instead of in his gap and bringing it all together. Once again, what we aim for in life starts with us—individually. So, let's break it down as Jesus did with the parable of the sower of the seeds. And when we look in the mirror, this could hurt!

1. Group 1 is those who have no aim or target—no goal in sight. This person has little interest or concern—no motivation or enthusiasm for anything, especially work or study. They want to stay in their comfort zone of complacency. They don't want to take any action—and for the most part they possess a negative and toxic mindset.

2. Group 2 is those who aim to set goals but fall short. In most cases, their goals were not specific (they were murky). Doubt sets in—they lack motivation, focus, and the desired commitment. In many cases, they blame others—not themselves. They have more excuses and scapegoats than you can fathom. They're easily distracted and give up way too soon!

3. Group 3 aims to please "oneself." They *seem* to be pointed in the right direction, armed, equipped, and ready—to achieve that *one* goal. Their drive is set on accomplishing the desired outcome that's *best suited for them*. Once "their" goal is achieved, they're done.

4. Group 4 are the special ones with the utmost of intentions, aiming at the highest mark, which means they are ambitious with a heart-driven determination to ensure that this objective is attained (no matter what). They are homed in, focused with all the diligence required. Yes, they know there will be obscuring things along the way that will distract them, but their intense passion, drive, and desire will have a good outcome for not just them—but others, as well. Their *faith* and willingness are second to none because they are focused on the "quality of the work"! *They possess an attitude of endurance and perseverance that leads them to press on for more!*

Which group do you belong in?

We must set our target on what matters to our Lord and Savior! And we must remind ourselves our goals cannot be attained *spiritually* if the world or our flesh consumes us! Paul reminded the believers in Rome that "They who are in the flesh cannot please God" (Rom 8:8).

When our hearts are pointed towards the Lord, equipped with his word, yielding to his Spirit, and possessing a genuine intention of wholehearted commitment, then we will know that our "real" target is in sight, which is aimed at pleasing our Heavenly Father! In your spiritual scope—are you homing in on the right target?

> And it is impossible to please God without faith. Anyone who wants to come to him must believe that God exists and that he rewards those who sincerely seek him. (Heb 11:6)

CHAPTER 7

His Presence

> When everything was ready, the Lord said to Noah, "Go into the boat with all your family, for among all the people of the earth, I can see that you alone are righteous." (Gen 7:1)

In this powerful passage, we see God telling Noah, "come into the ark." *In this profound moment, it's apparent God will be in the ark with them throughout the duration of the storm!* For 120 years, Noah was committed to God, obeyed him, and believed him, and he did not waver from his trust in God. This should simply remind us God will always be with those who are committed to him—wholeheartedly.

Noah did not take his family into the ark until God called him, but what a gracious and beautiful invitation from God to enter his place of safety and refuge. Noah must have felt such a level of comfort knowing the Almighty One would be in their presence, leading them every step of the way in this 377-day journey.

Today, Christians possess God's presence through his indwelling Holy Spirit (John 16:13; Rom 8:9), which comes from faith in our Lord Jesus Christ. We recognize his company through our obedience to his word and the power of the Holy Spirit in our lives. And His existing power reveals the status of our Almighty God as omnipotent, omnipresent, and omniscient!

When we're grounded in the principles of God's word, fellowshipping with other believers, yearning to grow closer to him, praying without ceasing, and seeking godly counsel, we feel it! We realize in the very depths of our soul and spirit, His Spirit is enabling us to live our new life!

A comforting thought to remember is that we never lose the reality of God's presence; for God's word tells us that we can't be separated from his love (Rom 8:31–39)—no matter how badly we mess up. Regardless of the depths of our sins, as true believers, we cannot lose our salvation and the presence of the Holy Spirit.

Can we anger God because of our sinful and rebellious ways? Yes! But as his faithful followers, we never lose his presence. We might lose that human "sense or feeling" of his presence when the harmful vices of this world and our flesh consume us. But here's the key—as his children, we are aware of the reality of God's presence through our continued faithfulness and obedience to his word.

When we get caught up in the sinful desires of our flesh, we start to feel a disconnect from our Heavenly Father—and absent from his presence. In our life, there will be times when we'll experience spiritual weakness when the Lord determines to test our faith. But here's his amazing love for us—he pushes us through those fiery flames of pain and suffering so that we might be pure and stronger for his glory (1 Pet 1:7)!

The benefit of being in God's presence is his absolute joy on display in our daily life! The power of the Holy Spirit's conviction and counsel will constantly reassure you of his presence: "The joy of the Lord is your strength" (Neh 8:10).

James, the Lord's brother, writes, "Dear brothers and sisters, when troubles of any kind come your way, consider it an opportunity for great joy" (Jas 1:2). When we endure and persevere through troublesome times, proving to ourselves and others that our faith is genuine, our sense of God's presence increases—as does our joy.

> You will show me the way of life, granting me the joy of your presence and the pleasures of living with you forever. (Ps 16:11)

CHAPTER 8

Pleasing to God

> Then Noah built an altar to the Lord, and there he sacrificed as burnt offerings the animals and birds that had been approved for that purpose. And the Lord was pleased with the aroma of the sacrifice and said to himself, "I will never again curse the ground because of the human race, even though everything they think or imagine is bent toward evil from childhood. I will never again destroy all living things." . . . Then God blessed Noah and his sons and told them, "Be fruitful and multiply. Fill the earth." (Gen 8:20–21; 9:1)

Noah's first act of business after God told them to leave the boat was powerful. He came out (after spending over a year in this vessel) and worshiped God! He built an altar to the Lord and sacrificed animals and birds "that had been approved for that purpose." The Lord was pleased with the aroma and sacrifice and even said to himself, "I will never again curse the earth destroying all living things . . . even though people's thoughts and actions are bent towards evil from childhood!" God knows we'll let him down at some point in our life, but he still showers us with his amazing love, grace, and mercy!

Noah's act is a beautiful depiction of authentic and genuine worship. No matter the storms in our life, the condition of our worship should mirror Noah's, which was a sweet aroma and pleasing in the sight of God! If ours is not genuine, do we think it's acceptable to our Lord?

Unfortunately, it seems we set conditions on when and how we want to worship and praise the Almighty Creator—ouch. I'm pointing this out as much to me as anyone else. God blessed Noah (and his sons) after his genuine and approved sacrifice because it was one of gratitude, thanking God for their salvation during the ultimate storm of life. Noah was dedicating the beginning of a new creation to his Heavenly Father.

Our sacrifices today should be from the core of our hearts with genuine love and devotion to our Lord Jesus Christ (Luke 10:27). We should sacrifice our mouth, tongue, and choice of deeds and words and let them be pleasing and honoring to him (Jas 3:1–12). We should be a living sacrifice (Rom 12:1), showing gratefulness to God by being "dead to self" and allowing him to use us in ways of service that glorify him.

Unfortunately, many of us are hanging on to some old hangers stored up in the worldly closets that we need to hand over to the Lord. Those ugly hangers, such as pride and "our" will, prevent us from living a life pleasing to God! But when we submit these vices over and allow God's Spirit to fine-tune us—it opens us up for genuine repentance and cleansing, which is pleasing to God! He wants that spiritual cleaning for all of us. "The sacrifice you desire is a broken spirit. You will not reject a broken and repentant heart, O God" (Ps 51:17).

Pleasing God means living according to his word and doing so in love and obedience. *Naturally, we want to please those we love, right?* The New Testament is full of encouraging ways to righteous living and loving Christ by obeying him daily. "If you love me, obey my commandments" (John 14:15). And it is by these acts of obedience that we please our Lord.

First Thessalonians 2:12 says, "We pleaded with you, encouraged you, and urged you to live your lives in a way that God would consider worthy. For he called you to share in his Kingdom and glory." And to think we've been given the unbelievable opportunity and chance to share these words of hope with others, and there's nothing more pleasing—it's priceless!

> And so, dear brothers and sisters, I plead with you to give your bodies to God because of all he has done for you. Let them be a living and holy sacrifice—the kind he will find acceptable. This is truly the way to worship him. (Rom 12:1)

CHAPTER 9

He Promises

Then God said, "I am giving you a sign of my covenant with you and with all living creatures, for all generations to come. I have placed my rainbow in the clouds. It is the sign of my covenant with you and with all the earth. When I send clouds over the earth, the rainbow will appear in the clouds, and I will remember my covenant with you and with all living creatures. Never again will the floodwaters destroy all life. When I see the rainbow in the clouds, I will remember the eternal covenant between God and every living creature on earth." Then God said to Noah, "Yes, this rainbow is the sign of the covenant I am confirming with all the creatures on earth." (Gen 9:12–17)

In chapter 9, there were powerful words between God and Noah and his sons. He reaffirms that he is giving a promise to mankind and he will never again flood the earth. God even says this sign will remind him of His promise he made to Noah and his sons and "all generations to come." Yes, this includes you and me.

God, in all his mercy and grace, says on at least two occasions he "will remember." He only had to tell Noah and his sons once, but God repeated it several times. This is a wonderful reminder that God commits to us through his word he will protect us not once but always. He is indeed a God of love and faithfulness.

The earth's order and seasons are preserved with the command of his word, and we have his promise that the rainbow, which is still visible today, is his promise to sustain us. What a wonderful reminder of his promise today.

Intriguingly, many myths explain the rainbow as some supernatural "bridge." But the most important theme is that the rainbow illustrates God's gracious and grand purpose of redemption. He not only spared Noah and his family, but also gave humanity yet another chance to start anew. Experts say rainbows contain a continuum of around one million colors indistinguishable from the human eye. Instead, we can only see seven colors: red, orange, yellow, green, blue, indigo, and violet. A rainbow is not much more than an "optical illusion." It only appears when a viewer is looking from just the right angle relative to the light source. And here's another powerful point: *some of the brightest rainbows appear after the darkest storms*!

When facing a challenge and thinking everything is going wrong, remember God has a joy-filled rainbow waiting to shine brightly for you and me. When we look at God's masterpiece and promise *just the right way*, it should remind us we've been given another chance, and that opportunity still stands today.

As a chaplain, preacher, and teacher in the prison ministry, I remember posing this one question to all the inmates in a group session one night. "If you were given the opportunity to choose one word that could make all the difference in your life moving forward, what would it be?" It was almost unanimous the one word was "chance." They wanted one chance to heal their past broken promises and make things right moving forward.

Their failed promises led to a heavy load that they've carried for years, preventing them from living a life of spiritual freedom. In a decisive spiritual moment, I told them they would get their chance to make things right and heal those broken promises, but that one chance would hinge on their *choice to change*.

God's promise is freely available for anyone who chooses his Son, Jesus Christ today. He will give anyone a chance, but their promise to the Father is that they will change their ways and follow his Son (John 3:16–17).

> For all of God's promises have been fulfilled in Christ with a resounding "Yes!" And through Christ, our "Amen" (which means "Yes") ascends to God for his glory. (2 Cor 1:20)

CHAPTER 10

Don't Rebel

> Cush was also the ancestor of Nimrod, who was the first heroic warrior on earth. Since he was the greatest hunter in the world, his name became proverbial. People would say, "This man is like Nimrod, the greatest hunter in the world." He built his kingdom in the land of Babylonia, with the cities of Babylon, Erech, Akkad, and Calneh. (Gen 10:8–10)

There's not a lot known about Nimrod; he's one of the most mysterious men in God's word. Besides what God states in His word, he was a mighty warrior and hunter with great gifts; and he was Noah's great grandson. The kingdoms he possessed were probably either started from the ground up or conquered. Therefore, in this passage, we can ascertain that he was probably a *hunter of men* since he was a mighty warrior and built kingdoms.

The historian Josephus said this about Nimrod: "He would be revenged on God, if he should have a mind to drown the world again; for he would build a tower too high for the waters to be able to reach and that he would avenge himself on God for destroying their forefathers." The motive, according to Josephus, for building the Tower of Babel was to protect humanity against another flood. But the reason for the first flood was humanity's wickedness and rebellion (Gen 6:5–6), in which humankind refused to repent and turn to God. So regardless of what a good deal may say, Nimrod was rebellious against God.[1]

Rebellion is opposition to authority, and it can lead to violent acts. And against the proper authority, it is a serious matter in the eyes of God. We all have this seed of rebellion because of our ugly, sinful nature. When we feel someone is not respecting our rights, in many cases, we rebel. But what

1. Roat, "7 Facts," para. 25.

should be our proper course of action? Obedience to God's word and heeding his Spirit's guidance will always be the spiritual choice and path to take.

When the presence of his Spirit is leading us—and it's evident to others, we learn to appeal to our authorities and leaders in ways that would avoid rebellion, but still find a peaceful resolution to a problem. Remember, as Christians, we represent Christ—so we must continually allow the power of God's word and his Spirit to establish his ways within us—where we can channel our passions and desires for change in productive Christlike ways.

We should be godly examples in times like today, offering solutions in respectful and honorable ways, such as the prophet Daniel. When you look at the model of this great prophet, he worked diligently and respectfully under several kingdoms. Daniel's exemplary acts of hope, trust, patience, and humility were evidence of Who his "true Leader and Guide" was, especially when dealing with different personalities. It's always pleasing to the Lord when we take the route of humility versus aggression.

We must realize in today's culture we're always going to have difficult people who disagree with us and try to upset us and steal our peace and joy. But we don't have to respond to every critical person in our life. We can all take the high road and give it to the Lord! God's word reminds us in Prov 17:28, "Even fools are thought wise when they keep silent; with their mouths shut, they seem intelligent."

Let's face it—*many people today don't want peace*—they want to fight, rebel, and be defiant. God's word tells us in Luke 10:5-6 that when Jesus sent his disciples to specific homes, he told them always to speak peace over those homes. And then he said, in effect, "If they are not peaceful, the blessing will return to you." That's comforting—they may not accept peace, but he reassures me if I am at rest in him, I will have peace. When we do the right thing, God will see it and reward it—especially when we're sowing "good seeds" for his glory in this rebellious world (see Gal chapter 6)!

> Evil people are eager for rebellion, but they will be severely punished. (Prov 17:11)

WEEK 3

His Covenant—Our Commitment

Gen 11–15

In week 3 (chapters 11–15), we start to see God's plan for his chosen ones come to fruition. However, some rebels thought they could build a monument more significant than God—in an attempt to draw attention to themselves. Still, man's plan would fail again, and God would set out to make a promise for the ages—setting apart his holy ones from the rest of the world.

The Abrahamic promise in Gen 12 is probably the most significant portion of Genesis and the center of the Pentateuch. God reveals three elements in this promise: land, descendants, and a divine-human relationship. The Abrahamic covenant signifies a permanent central point in the direction of Genesis. Before this passage, there was a repetitive theme of sin destroying God's creation. It seems that humankind tends to destroy what God has made good.

While God makes an unbelievable promise with Abraham that sets the course of time, he expects our total commitment to him through his Son, Jesus. The latter is our sole authority, our guiding light, and our accurate compass in life. Committing to Christ means being fruitful—a dedicated servant to his cause. "For to me, living means living for Christ, and dying is even better" (Phil 1:21). Every fiber should be committed to loving and serving our Lord. It's not a part-time job where you get full-time benefits; it's a full-time job where you get eternal rewards. Paul said, "I have been crucified with Christ. It is no longer I who live, but Christ who lives in me. And the life I now live in the flesh I live by faith in the Son of God, who loved me and gave Himself for me" (Gal 2:20). Commit to the Lord your willingness to deny self each day and follow his ways—daily.

CHAPTER 11

Godly Accomplisher

> Then they said, "Come, let's build a great city for ourselves with a tower that reaches into the sky. This will make us famous and keep us from being scattered all over the world." But the Lord came down to look at the city and the tower the people were building. "Look!" he said. "The people are united, and they all speak the same language. After this, nothing they set out to do will be impossible for them! Come, let's go down and confuse the people with different languages. Then they won't be able to understand each other." In that way, the Lord scattered them all over the world, and they stopped building the city. (Gen 11:4–8)

"Let's tell the whole world how famous we are," they said. "Let's make a name for ourselves to be remembered in our honor for generations to come. We will build a city and tower that will make us great—this will be 'our' plan to keep us together and prevent us from being scattered. *"Oh! what a tangled web we weave / When first we practise[sic] to deceive."*[1] *When we lie, mislead, or simply dishonest, our actions could lead to a domino effect of problems and complications that can spiral out of control.* What little did these rebels know—because of their defiance—God would use it to bring together his worldwide plan.

After the flood, God instructed Noah and his sons to be fruitful, multiply, and fill the earth. And over the course of time—there was a failure to communicate God's intentional plan because the future generation did the absolute opposite by building an enormous tower of "their" greatness and human achievement. It was a monument built to honor themselves, not God—even after he gave humans another chance. Their unity was of

---

1. Scott, *Marmion*, 7.17.

themselves—because their self-accomplishments, goals, and pride had no intentions of honoring God!

God confused their languages, so they could no longer communicate with each other. The result was that people congregated with others who spoke the same language and then went out together and settled in other parts of the world (Gen 11:8–9). God confused them to enforce his command for humanity to spread across the world.

Today's languages still serve as a dividing point in our culture. The Tower of Babel is an excellent depiction of how God can intervene and obliterate our plans when they don't include him. He can bring us to the realization that our main line of communication should always be with and through him.

So many people today want to make "their own" mark in the communities, churches, schools, local government, states, and globally. They want to be remembered for their achievements because that's the measure of their legacy. And unfortunately, we have our monuments in life that we honor and sometimes place ahead of God. Whether personal possessions, accolades, notoriety, success, or money, they can sometimes get in the way of glorifying God. And after all, isn't he the One that's blessed us with these accomplishments?

We need to remember there's nothing wrong with accomplishments and having nice things, "but" if that's how the world identifies us, we're pegged more to the worldly things—than those that honor God. What are we building in our spiritual life? Is God part of the blueprints? As you sketch out your plans—always take them to the Lord (Prov 16:3).

We are free to do as we want, but for every wrong decision, there are consequences. If God is not part of the original plan, do we really expect him to honor it? Attain his approval as you move forward and ensure it's his will through prayer, his word, and other firm believers in Christ. *And in his timing,* it will be accomplished—all for his glory.

> If you keep yourself pure, you will be a special utensil for honorable use. Your life will be clean, and you will be ready for the Master to use you for every good work. (2 Tim 2:21)

CHAPTER 12

All In

> One day Terah took his son Abram, his daughter-in-law Sarai (his son Abram's wife), and his grandson Lot (his son Haran's child) and moved away from Ur of the Chaldeans. He was headed for the land of Canaan, but they stopped at Haran and settled there. Terah lived for 205 years and died while still in Haran. . . . "Leave your native country, your relatives, and your father's family, and go to the land that I will show you. I will make you into a great nation. I will bless you and make you famous and be a blessing to others. I will bless those who bless you and curse those who treat you with contempt. All families on earth will be blessed through you." (Gen 11:31–32; 12:1–2)

Terah left Ur of the Chaldeans, a thriving ancient city in its day, and never made it to the land of Canaan. On his journey, he would wander and *stop approximately halfway* in a village named Haran. After all, Terah's name in Hebrew means "wanderer." Could it have been he was ill or simply tired of traveling? Because Haran is where he would dwell for his remaining years on earth.

Joshua 24:2–3 provides us a snapshot of the life of Terah; he was an idol maker, and idol worshiper. God knew Terah would not make the complete journey, for his faith was in other gods. But it would set the stage for a man who would be blessed and made famous by God, one that would be a blessing to others, the father of many nations, and all the families would be blessed through him. Although Abram's father (Terah) was an idol worshiper and only made it *halfway*, God would use his son (Abram) for great things because of his undeniable faith.

Abram (soon to be renamed Abraham) plays an essential role in Christianity. Through his lineage, the Savior of the world would come (Matt

1; Luke 3). Abram was the first man chosen by God for a role in the plan of redemption. He was chosen to be the father of many nations—because it was God's will. God knew Abram would struggle with the call set before him, but he also foreknew his struggle would produce significant growth and faith. And this is what God wants to build in us today (2 Pet 1:5–11).

Abram's faith was steadfast in God regardless of his weak areas. So, when God told him to take his family and leave home and go to another land, he went without knowing where he was going; he obeyed God without questioning his command!

When we yield to our steadfast faith in God and allow his Spirit to lead us, he will see you and me through the journey "all the way," not just halfway. What a blessing when God can call anyone, regardless of their ancestral past, to live a life for him and be a part of his grand plan. But we mustn't be halfway Christians in a world today that needs to *see the wholeness of our Savior!*

Being "all in" means we are ready and willing to give our all for him—go wherever and do whatever we are called to do. In Mark 8:35–37, Jesus said this: "If you try to hang on to your life, you will lose it. But if you give up your life for my sake and for the sake of the Good News, you will save it. And what do you benefit if you gain the whole world but lose your own soul? Is anything worth more than your soul?"

In one of my mentoring sessions in prison, I recall a time when an inmate was trying to make a change in his life for Christ. He told me one day, *"I can't do this anymore; the enemy has tormented me since I started this journey."* I looked at him and said, *"So you want full-time benefits but only to offer the Lord part-time services?"* It doesn't work that way—he's called us to be *"all in for him—all the way!"*

Here is the perseverance of his saints who keep the commandments of God and their faith in Jesus all the way— *"This means that God's holy people must endure persecution patiently, obeying his commands and maintaining their faith in Jesus"* (Rev 14:12). Until that day of glory!

CHAPTER 13

Right Perspective

Lot, who was traveling with Abram, had also become very wealthy with flocks of sheep and goats, herds of cattle, and many tents. But the land could not support both Abram and Lot with all their flocks and herds living so close together. So, disputes broke out between the herdsmen of Abram and Lot. (At that time Canaanites and Perizzites were also living in the land.)

Finally, Abram said to Lot, "Let's not allow this conflict to come between us or our herdsmen. After all, we are close relatives! The whole countryside is open to you. Take your choice of any section of the land you want, and we will separate. If you want the land to the left, then I'll take the land on the right. If you prefer the land on the right, then I'll go to the left."

Lot took a long look at the fertile plains of the Jordan Valley in the direction of Zoar. The whole area was well watered everywhere, like the garden of the LORD or the beautiful land of Egypt. (This was before the LORD destroyed Sodom and Gomorrah.) Lot chose for himself the whole Jordan Valley to the east of them. He went there with his flocks and servants and parted company with his uncle Abram. So, Abram settled in the land of Canaan, and Lot moved his tents to a place near Sodom and settled among the cities of the plain. But the people of this area were extremely wicked and constantly sinned against the LORD.

After Lot had gone, the LORD said to Abram, "Look as far as you can see in every direction—north and south, east and west. I am giving all this land, as far as you can see, to you and your descendants as a permanent possession. And I will give you so many descendants that, like the dust of the earth, they cannot be counted!" (Gen 13:5–16)

You could write a powerful book and movie from these profound verses. Facing a potential conflict with Lot, Abram took the initiative (he took the first step) to make things right. He gave Lot the first choice, even though Abram had the right to choose first as the elder. Abram could see there was petty jealousy tearing them apart. Lot was wealthy in his own right because of Abram's blessings from God. But one party involved in this matter wanted more of the riches for themself.

Lot's true character is revealed in his choice! But look at the power of what God's word says in verse 11. After Lot chose the land for "himself," which he saw as fertile from his own eyes, what little did he know was the evil lurking ahead beyond the horizon in Sodom. As many would say, *the pasture is not always greener on the other side.*

God blesses Abram even more because of his Godly character. The words that Abram conveyed to Lot, "take your choice of any section of the land you want," are the exact words God spoke to Abram (after Lot left). Still, God said, "look as far as you can see in every direction (north, south, east, and west), for I am giving all this land as far as you can see to you and your descendants as a 'permanent' possession." Abram's godly character is shown in his actions—for he gave Lot the first choice. He resolved the conflict and put family peace above personal desires.

Life is a series of choices almost daily. What we think is a good choice because it looks good from our "own" perspective will often lead to problems. When our heart and motives are not in line with the nature of God, "our" sense of direction will be off course. Fertile land seemed like a wise choice (through Lot's eyes). Still, he failed to see the lurking and working of Sodom's evil temptations that were strong enough to destroy his own family. God commands us to reach people like those in Sodom, but we must be careful not to get tangled up with the lifestyles of the wicked that can separate us from the will of God!

When our perspectives are more in view of the world, it has the power to change our behavior from the "right way" of looking at things. And that wrong perspective can reframe our thought process and transform our lives into worldly positions that are not pleasing to God. So today, more than ever, we need to take time, clear our spiritual lenses, and lean on his word and Spirit to view life from a higher perspective that is more in tune with the ways of God.

> So we don't look at the troubles we can see now; rather, we fix
> our gaze on things that cannot be seen. For the things we see

now will soon be gone, So we don't look at the troubles we can see now; rather, we fix our gaze on things that cannot be seen. For the things we see now will soon be gone, but the things we cannot see will last forever. (2 Cor 4:18)

CHAPTER 14

Our Helper

> When Abram heard that his nephew Lot had been captured, he mobilized the 318 trained men who had been born into his household. Then he pursued Kedorlaomer's army until he caught up with them at Dan. There he divided his men and attacked during the night. Kedorlaomer's army fled, but Abram chased them as far as Hobah, north of Damascus. Abram recovered all the goods that had been taken, and he brought back his nephew Lot with his possessions and all the women and other captives. (Gen 14:14–16)

Abram was a man who walked by faith, yet he was also a wise and cautious man. He kept his army, trained and ready to defend his interests. Abram's army pursued the confederacy of four kings for a long distance to the north. With God's help, they conquered Kedorlaomer's army and rescued Lot.

Lot's greed led him into sinful surroundings and desires for more materialistic possessions, success, and wealth. And this would cost him his freedom, and then he faced slavery, torture, and possible death. What a price to pay when we pursue the wrong things in life.

Wrong choices can lead us into areas of our lives that have danger written all over them. So many deceiving things in this world can entice us, entangle us, and enslave us in a world far away from our Lord.

But when we submit our unhealthy ways to the Lord, he will come and rescue us because He is always prepared to get us out of a mess or painful situation. But to reciprocate, we should also be ready as believers to help others in serious need—as Abram did for Lot. After all, that's what our Lord expects from each one of his true followers!

Psalm 46:1–2 reminds us that he's our refuge and strength and always ready to help us in times of trouble, but the key point is the proceeding verse, which should always be our response—"So, we will not fear!" If our faith is entirely steadfast in him, we should always rest and know that our Lord wants us to sit down, be quiet, take rest, trust him, and know that he's got us in the palm of his hands!

God's word reminds us in Ps 18:17–21, "He rescued me from my powerful enemies, from those who hated me and were too strong for me. They attacked me at a moment when I was in distress, but the Lord supported me. He led me to a place of safety; He rescued me because He delights in me. *The Lord rewarded me for doing right; He restored me because of my innocence. For I have kept the ways of the Lord; I have not turned from my God to follow evil.*"[1]

When you feel you're at your wit's end, at the end of your rope, or drowning in your troubles, remember that God is there to help. Still, the key is nestled in this passage: *"The Lord rewards those for doing right."*

God loves a reciprocating heart—one that returns the favor with a kind and genuine spirit. First Peter 2:9 reminds us, "But you are not like that, for you are a chosen people. You are royal priests, a holy nation, God's very own possession. As a result, you can show others the goodness of God, for he called you out of the darkness into his wonderful light." He's our Faithful Helper, but he also expects us to be *faithful to him* and others, too.

> Don't be afraid, for I am with you. Don't be discouraged, for I am your God. I will strengthen you and help you. I will hold you up with my victorious right hand. (Isa 41:10)

---

1. My emphasis.

CHAPTER 15

Transparent with God

> Sometime later, the LORD spoke to Abram in a vision and said to him, "Do not be afraid, Abram, for I will protect you, and your reward will be great." But Abram replied, "O Sovereign LORD, what good are all your blessings when I don't even have a son? Since you've given me no children, Eliezer of Damascus, a servant in my household, will inherit all my wealth. You have given me no descendants of my own, so one of my servants will be my heir." Then the LORD said to him, "No, your servant will not be your heir, for you will have a son of your own who will be your heir." Then the LORD took Abram outside and said to him, "Look up into the sky and count the stars if you can. That's how many descendants you will have!" And Abram believed the LORD, and the LORD counted him as righteous because of his faith. Then the LORD told him, "I am the LORD who brought you out of Ur of the Chaldeans to give you this land as your possession." (Gen 15:1–5)

You have to love the transparency between God and Abram—for Abram spoke from his heart concerned about the lineage of his heir, as he had no children, which was huge! But God tells him he will have an heir, and "Abram believed" because he had absolute trust in God. This is even quoted in the New Testament by Paul and James, establishing that *Abram's faith made him right with God.*

While we all know that Abram was not perfect (for no one is), we must understand the key to staying right with God as transparent and faithful Christians. First, it is a matter of our heart—recognizing what he has done for us through his Son Jesus. We must acknowledge our flaws and sinful ways, as we will see in the next chapter with Abram. Finally, we all must realize that sin is what separates from God's will, and it can prevent us from being transparent with the Lord in all areas of our life!

We need to approach his throne of love, mercy, and grace with an open heart and realize "there is no one who does good, not even one" (Ps 14:3). He wants a pure and genuine heart in his presence—with no level of pride.

When we're all in as believing Christians, we hold nothing back from our Savior! Our humble confession and turning to God will put us on the right track to a proper relationship, just like Abram had with God. When we're open with God, it's coming from an authentic heart that recognizes their need for help, and they need to pour it all out to the Almighty One!

Don't be fooled—*when you want to conceal and not reveal things to the Lord, that's the enemy holding you back, because he doesn't want us to recognize our errs, for that is when he's on the prowl and blindsides us.* The enemy does not want us to disclose our flaws to the Lord—he wants us to bottle them up inside, so we will have an implosion. He wants to steal our peace and joy, and he wants us to live an unsatisfied life! But the Lord has more for you and me when we come before his presence with an open and genuine heart!

Fear not, don't be afraid, I am your shield, I will always be with you, I will protect you, and your reward will be great—these are all encouraging words we need to remember from our faithful God. His protection is enough to eliminate all our fears. Why? Because he's with us, beside us, goes ahead of us, shields us, leads us, and wants to bless us!

Like Abram, we must choose to have a solid, open, faithful, and loving relationship with our Sovereign God. *He does not hold back anything that will help us. His words are an open book that we can always trust (Ps 84:11)!*

The only way toward a genuine and open relationship with God is to trust him in all areas of our life and know that he's our Sustainer! Although we may not see changes immediately, we will over time. And that was clear in Abram's life. It took time, but as always—God comes through with his master plan! *So, let go—and let God be God!*

> Work hard so you can present yourself to God and receive his approval. Be a good worker, one who does not need to be ashamed and who correctly explains the word of truth. (2 Tim 2:15)

WEEK 4

SEEK & FIND

Gen 16–20

In week 4 (chapters 16–20), we will start to experience our actual wants in life. If the Lord gave you a piece of paper and asked you to list all your desires, would they line up with his perfect will, purpose, and plan for your life?

Seeking the Lord first sets forth our true priorities; it shows what is essential in our life. Many people know the famous passage in Jer 29:11. Still, they don't quote the passage proceeding in verses 12 and 13 on God's requirements, "In those days when you pray, I will listen. If you look for me wholeheartedly, you will find Me." The key here is when we seek the Lord with all of our hearts.

God's word reminds us in Matt 6:33, "Seek the Kingdom of God above all else, and live righteously, and he will give you everything you need." In other words—our primary concern is we have a strong desire to have a deeper understanding of God's wisdom and to grasp his knowledge in everything he does. It's not an occasional thing; it's an everyday commitment. Does this mean we will have all the answers? No! But little by little, through that growing process, we're picking up more and more things with clarity.

Christians utilizing every opportunity to seek and find Christ first have a heart-set focused on Him. He's their number-one priority, nothing else. God's business should be a top priority in our everyday life! We should seek his salvation, live in obedience to him, and share his good news with others. Then he will take care of our business as he promised. There's no need to worry!

In Celebrate Recovery, they share testimonies on the hurts, habits, and hang-ups in their life. They will tell you through it all, when you act upon your convictions, seek his counsel, and rest in his comfort, you've found the One who can lead you into all Truths. And that's a basic principle we need in our everyday life. Sometimes we need to be in the lowest places of our lives to seek and find the One True Light who can bring us out of our darkest and most despaired times.

CHAPTER 16

Seek His Counsel

Now Sarai, Abram's wife, had not been able to bear children for him. But she had an Egyptian servant named Hagar. So, Sarai said to Abram, "The Lord has prevented me from having children. Go and sleep with my servant. Perhaps I can have children through her." And Abram agreed with Sarai's proposal. So, Sarai, Abram's wife, took Hagar the Egyptian servant and gave her to Abram as a wife. (This happened ten years after Abram had settled in the land of Canaan.)

So, Abram had sexual relations with Hagar, and she became pregnant. But when Hagar knew she was pregnant, she began to treat her mistress, Sarai, with contempt. Then Sarai said to Abram, "This is all your fault! I put my servant into your arms, but now that she's pregnant she treats me with contempt. The Lord will show who's wrong—you or me!" Abram replied, "Look, she is your servant, so deal with her as you see fit." Then Sarai treated Hagar so harshly that she finally ran away. The angel of the Lord found Hagar beside a spring of water in the wilderness, along the road to Shur. The angel said to her, "Hagar, Sarai's servant, where have you come from, and where are you going?" "I'm running away from my mistress, Sarai," she replied. The angel of the Lord said to her, "Return to your mistress, and submit to her authority." Then he added, "I will give you more descendants than you can count." (Gen 16:1–10)

Indeed, you would have thought Abram "believed" God in chapter 15, when God said, "That you would have an heir of your own," he knew this heir was of him and Sarai. But he got all caught up in Sarai's frustration and impatience when Sarai said, "The Lord has prevented me from having children—go and sleep with my servant." You would think that Abram, the spiritual and faithful leader, would have shared with his wife; "Wait—this is what the Lord has told me, we would have an heir of our own." Men, we should learn from this lesson.

Look at what can happen when our minds wander. The flesh takes over, and these vices surface—impatient and conspiring acts, division, anger, jealousy, pride, contempt, unaccountability, discord, and ultimately the lack of focus on God's plan. Where did Sarai come up with the thought; "God has prevented me from having children"? Is she holding the Lord responsible for her inability to bear children? In her mind, he is the one preventing this from happening. Maybe God was doing that—executing his plan in his timing. Sarai, though, didn't want to wait any longer, for she would take matters into her own hands.

Seeking the counsel of our Lord and praying for his wisdom, discernment, and guidance will minimize the enemy's work in our daily life. For example, look at what happened with the three prominent people in this chapter when they didn't take things to the Lord. *Sarai* took matters into her own hands when confronting *Abram*, who went along with the plan. And when all went wrong, Abram refused to get involved and solve the problem (did you see the shifting of blame between Sarai and Abram?). And then *Hagar* ran away from the situation.

The enemy attacks when we allow him to plant seeds of doubt, discontent, and discouragement in our minds. It leads us to take matters into our own hands and get off course. But our Almighty and Sovereign God always comes to the rescue when we mess things up. Even though we are discontent, impatient, and concoct our own plans, he loves us so much that he steps in with the power of his grace to assist. God demonstrated his ability to work in all things for the good (Rom 8:28).

Later, God gave Abram and Sarai the son they wanted, and God solved Hagar's problem even though Abram did not assist. When we allow God to help us with patience and contentment, He will come through. Seeking God's advice will always bring clarity—in his timing.

> Plans go wrong for lack of advice; many advisers bring success.
> (Prov 15:22)

CHAPTER 17

Inward Change

> "I will confirm my covenant with you and your descendants after you, from generation to generation. This is the everlasting covenant: I will always be your God and the God of your descendants after you. And I will give the entire land of Canaan, where you now live as a foreigner, to you and your descendants. It will be their possession forever, and I will be their God." Then God said to Abraham, "Your responsibility is to obey the terms of the covenant. You and all your descendants have this continual responsibility." (Gen 17:7–9)

Earlier in chapter 17, God makes a covenant with Abram (a promise between two or more parties) and changes his name from Abram (exalted father) to Abraham (father of many nations). He says to Abram, "Serve me faithfully and live a blameless life." God tells Abraham that he will continue this everlasting covenant between us, generation after generation, and between God and Abraham's offspring forever. He will be Abraham's God and the God of his descendants after him.

But here's the key in verse 9: God tells Abraham, "Your part of the agreement is to obey the terms of the covenant—you and your descendants have this *continual responsibility*." Does this apply to us today?

As 2 Tim 3:16–17 tells us, "All Scripture is inspired by God and is useful to teach us what is true and to make us realize what is wrong in our lives. It corrects us when we are wrong and teaches us to do what is right. God uses it to prepare and equip his people to do every good work." So, what is a nugget we can take away from Gen 17?

God required circumcision as a sign of obedience and belonging to his covenant—it symbolized the cutting off the old life of sin, purifying one's heart, and dedicating oneself to God. Once circumcised, there was no turning back because circumcision, more than any other practice, separated God's people from the pagan world.

Physical circumcision does not make one a child of God; faith does. Believers in Jesus Christ can say they are children of "Father Abraham." "If you belong to Christ, then you are Abraham's seed, and heirs according to the promise" (Galatians 3:29).

God has always wanted more from His people than just external conformity to a set of rules. He has always wanted them to possess a heart to love, know, and follow Him. That's why God is not concerned with the circumcision of the flesh. Even in the Old Testament, God's priority was a spiritual circumcision of the heart: "Circumcise yourselves to the LORD, circumcise your hearts, you men of Judah and people of Jerusalem, or my wrath will break out and burn like fire because of the evil you have done" (Jeremiah 4:4).[1]

That inward change should lead to a boldness and confidence to share the wonderful promise of the Good News with everyone (nothing should hold us back). A genuine relationship with Christ will permeate and radiate our assurance that He's alive in and through us.

> That is why we never give up. Though our bodies are dying, our spirits are being renewed every day. (2 Cor 4:16)

---

1. "What Is Circumcision of the Heart?," paras. 6–7.

CHAPTER 18

God Knows

"Where is Sarah, your wife?" the visitors asked. "She's inside the tent," Abraham replied. Then one of them said, "I will return to you about this time next year, and your wife, Sarah, will have a son!" Sarah was listening to this conversation from the tent. Abraham and Sarah were both very old by this time, and Sarah was long past the age of having children. So, she laughed silently to herself and said, "How could a worn-out woman like me enjoy such pleasure, especially when my master—my husband—is also so old?" Then the LORD said to Abraham, "Why did Sarah laugh? Why did she say, 'Can an old woman like me have a baby?' Is anything too hard for the LORD? I will return about this time next year, and Sarah will have a son." Sarah was afraid, so she denied it, saying, "I didn't laugh. "But the LORD said, "No, you did laugh." (Gen 18:9–15)

I love this—the first question the three men asked, "Where is your wife, Sarah?" God knew Sarah had been barren her entire life and wanted a child of her own, and God recognized that, and together with Abraham, he would bless them. But Sarah laughed within herself, in the tent, thinking no one else knew.

But, to her surprise, her internal feelings are known to the Lord (the One who knows all). She finds that there is One present Who rises above the realm of nature—our Almighty Creator and Heavenly Father. In her confusion and terror, she denied she laughed. But the Lord—*Who sees within us*—says, "You did laugh," at least in the thought of her heart.

Did Sarah lie because she was afraid of being discovered? Or did Sarah laugh because of doubt, lack of human ability, discouragement, disappointment, jealousy, or anger? Yet, even with all this ugly baggage, she would come to believe. This powerful statement would get anyone's attention: "Is anything too hard for the LORD?" (Gen 18:14). Sarah is even noted in the hall of faith in Heb 11 because, over time, Sarah would come to have faith in the Lord and believe that all he said would come true. *God knows when the timing is just right!*

It is likely that fear led Sarah not to be honest; fear is one of the most common motives for lying. When we're worried that our innermost thoughts and emotions or our sinful ways will be exposed, lying is the counter to cover up the "real truth." But suppose we're not honest with ourselves in a proper examination (2 Cor 13:5). In that case, we will never be honest with the One who" already" knows it all.

When we hide a sin, it brings another one into our life. And here's a gut punch. When our flesh oppositely denies the truth in a particular matter—how do we expect to be honest with the One True God—Who already knows all things?

So often, when trying to cover up, we're either looking for "our own" justification or a scapegoat to cover the absolute truth! But to whom the Lord loves, he will rebuke, convict, silence, and bring to repentance. (Heb 12—God disciplines those he loves.)

God knows when we call out his name for help, when we rejoice, and when we're not honest. He knows when we don't take him seriously, for he knows our hearts. In Heb 4:12–13, God's word tells us he exposes our innermost thoughts and desires for who we are because nothing is hidden from God.

When we seek comfort and assurance during a difficult time in our life, our true faith and belief in the Almighty One will not be in vain! He will restore, renew, refresh, and rebuild us to be like his Son! "And I am certain that God, who began the good work within you, will continue his work until it is finally finished on the day when Christ Jesus returns" (Phil 1:6).

> Nothing in all creation is hidden from God. Everything is naked and exposed before his eyes, and he is the one to whom we are accountable. (Heb 4:13)

CHAPTER 19

Desires Can Kill

> Meanwhile, the angels questioned Lot. "Do you have any other relatives here in the city?" they asked. "Get them out of this place—your sons-in-law, sons, daughters, or anyone else. For we are about to destroy this city completely. The outcry against this place is so great it has reached the LORD, and he has sent us to destroy it." So, Lot rushed out to tell his daughters' fiancés, "Quick, get out of the city! The LORD is about to destroy it." But the young men thought he was only joking. At dawn the next morning the angels became insistent. "Hurry," they said to Lot. "Take your wife and your two daughters who are here. Get out right now, or you will be swept away in the destruction of the city!" When Lot still hesitated, the angels seized his hand and the hands of his wife and two daughters and rushed them to safety outside the city, for the LORD was merciful. (Gen 19:12–16)

Homosexuality was part of why God destroyed the two cities because the men of Sodom and Gomorrah wanted to perform homosexual gang rape on the two angels (disguised as men; see 19:5). Still, we must not overlook what God told Abraham in chapter 18; God clearly says that *"Everything* they do is wicked and evil."

Ezekiel 16:49–50 declares, "Now this was the 'sin' of your sister Sodom: She and her daughters were arrogant-prideful, overfed and abundance of idleness; they did not help the poor and needy. They were 'haughty' and did detestable things before Me." "Detestable" refers to something morally disgusting and is the same word used in Lev 18:22 that refers to homosexuality as an "abomination."

So, from where does this sinful act stem? Remember a key and powerful verse that Jesus tells us in Matt 15:19–20, "That from the heart come evil thoughts, murder, adultery, "all" sexual immorality, theft, lying, and slander. These are what defile you." Our evil heart leads us to sin. Our hearts are so deceitful and evil that our motives can also be unclear to us. Jeremiah 17:9 even says, "The human heart is the most deceitful of all things, and desperately wicked. Who really knows how bad it is?"

And from an evil heart comes forth a sin so rooted that we cannot lose sight of it even in Sodom and Gomorrah (and us, as well), and that is sinful pride (haughtiness as quoted in Ezek 16:50). Pride can keep a person from accepting the ways of the Lord. It will prevent someone from acknowledging their sin, repenting, and turning to God because it's all about their way of life, not God's. Proverbs 16:25 says, "There is a way that seems right to a man, but its end is the way to death."

Pride can be a fountain of many sins because it's saying, "I want what I want, and I will have it regardless of what God says or even at the cost to someone else, because I am better than they are, and 'I' deserve it." Suppose that lustful passion is for "unusual flesh" or "unnatural desire," as Jude 1:7 describes it. In that case, that can lead to homosexual behavior. So yes, Sodom was judged for homosexual sin—which flowed from "pride," which also led to cruel and mistreating acts of their fellow men and women. What a domino effect of sinful acts!

It is easy for us to look at the story of Sodom and Gomorrah and point to that one act of evil—homosexuality—and not look at our own sin(s). But we must remind ourselves—at one time, we all have fallen snare to some level of pride in our lives.

Galatians 5 has been used by many who have led people to Christ, for it can scare the heebie-jeebies out of you. This chapter will help us all to realize God will not tolerate any sin that separates us from him. Galatians 5:19–21 says, "When you follow the desires of your sinful nature, the results are evident: sexual immorality, impurity, lustful pleasures, idolatry, sorcery, hostility, quarreling, jealousy, outbursts of anger, selfish ambition, dissension, division, envy, drunkenness, wild parties, and other sins like these. Again, as I have before, let me tell you that anyone living/practicing that sort of life will not inherit the Kingdom of God."

If the sinful desires mentioned here are routine, a typical behavior, habit, or a standard way of doing things, they are not good, and we must flee! The counter is delighting ourselves in what pleases the Lord and committing our all to His ways! In that case, he will not abandon us in our struggles and battles with sinful desires and tendencies, which separate us from his will and plan (1 Cor 10:13). Indeed, his love, mercy, grace, and patience are immeasurable for anyone, no matter who we are or what we've done.

The psalmist reminds us in Ps 37:4, "Take delight in the Lord, and he will give you your heart's desires." It's that undeniable righteous pursuit of his satisfactions and pleasures that are in accordance with his word and his ways. And when his word is our daily guide constructively, we know in the depths of our heart there's no deviation or variation. And most of all—we don't distort the words of his holiness to fit a lifestyle of ungodliness. We cling to the principles of God's teaching as our true source in life because we long to gratify him *first*—and as always, he will gratify us.

> So letting your sinful nature control your mind leads to death.
> But letting the Spirit control your mind leads to life and peace.
> (Rom 8:6)

CHAPTER 20

The Way Out

> [Abimelech said,] "Didn't Abraham tell me, 'She is my sister'? And she herself said, 'Yes, he is my brother.' I acted in complete innocence! My hands are clean." In the dream God responded, "Yes, I know you are innocent. That's why I kept you from sinning against me, and why I did not let you touch her. Now return the woman to her husband, and he will pray for you, for he is a prophet. Then you will live. But if you don't return her to him, you can be sure that you and all your people will die." (Gen 20:5–7)

Surely the father of all nations, the first patriarch, the loyal man of faith, founder of the Jewish nation, a man of hospitality, and one who tried to avoid conflicts was not up to his old tricks, again? But he was.

Once again, Abraham told Abimelech, to protect himself, that Sarah was his sister, not his wife. Now, it's true they were half-siblings, but still, Abraham is noted in this chapter for deceiving Abimelech and telling a *half-truth*. There's a point God is trying to show us in this passage.

Abraham acted out of fear because he lacked God's protection, which is a lack of faith. Still, also, he established a pattern of lying when he suspected his life was in danger and gave into this temptation because he did not trust God! In this story, Abraham thought it would be wise "in his mind" to deceive Abimelech rather than trust God to work in King Abimelech's life.

And let's note a half-truth is simply a way of manipulating something or someone in our favor. A good example is what Satan did to Eve in the garden, for he is the father of lies (John 8:44). Satan even quoted Scripture to Jesus with an attempt to mislead our Lord. What a sly and deceiving one he is—trying to manipulate us daily. Do we fall for it?

Undoubtedly, certain temptations are difficult for us all, no matter how much we love God and want to adhere to his holy word. When the enemy sees an open door, you can count on this; he will bust it down because we all have vulnerable areas of weakness in our spiritual armor (ouch). But it should encourage us that God is watching out for us—as you see in this story.

I love this part of the passage—God told Abimelech, "Yes, I know you are innocent; that's why I kept you from sinning." He kept him from sinning because the integrity of Abimelech's heart was right! In 1 Cor 10:12–13, Paul tells us, "If you think you are *standing firm*, be careful not to fall. The temptations in your life are no different from what others experience. And God is faithful. He will not allow the temptation to be more than you can stand."

So, when we're tempted, *he will show us a way out* so we can endure. What a great promise to know that our Faithful, Loving, Gracious, and Merciful God will not allow any temptation to be more than we can stand, but the key is this: recognize, resist, and flee from those weak areas, ask for his powering grace when they do come, always choose to do what is right "in his sight," and know that your most incredible Help is from the One Whose strength is made perfect in all of our weaknesses (2 Cor 12:9).

> Trust in the LORD with all your heart; do not depend on your understanding. Seek his will in all you do, and he will show you which path to take. (Prov 3:5–6)

WEEK 5

His Goodness Prevails

Gen 21–25

We're approaching the halfway point where we can taste God's Goodness and see the importance of real-life application. It is during these stages of development of resting in his assurance, allowing him to develop us, when we see those little things from a different perspective and realize that in every season, God's way is always right . . . it's always good!

God is good means that he has no evil in him, his intentions and motives are always good, he always does what is right, and the outcome of his plan is always good. There is nothing unpleasant about God—just think about that for a moment. With all the surrounding unpleasantries and negativities, evil intentions, and lack of pure motives, don't we need to dwell in the Goodness of God and know that through all our storms, he shall and will prevail? There's no greater hope than this—*what God has in store for us!* His Goodness should lead to our thankfulness each day.

As a living testimony we should exhibit his goodness throughout our lives—exemplifying His fruit of the Spirit where we've harbored selfishness, cruelty, rebelliousness, and hurt. We should reflect the character of God that relates directly to morality because it is virtue and holiness in action. It results in a life characterized by deeds motivated by righteousness and a desire to be a blessing to each person around us. It's the characteristic of a Spirit-filled person. Sounds daunting . . . but only through his power can we attain it for his glory!

CHAPTER 21

Rest Assured

> The LORD kept his word and did for Sarah exactly what he had promised. She became pregnant, and she gave birth to a son for Abraham in his old age. This happened at just the time God had said it would. (Gen 21:1–2)

God kept his promise to Abraham and Sarah, and "at just the right time," the lineage of redemption would continue through the birth of Isaac. It astonished Abraham and Sarah that they would bear a child at such an old age—but doing the impossible is part of God's everyday business.

There's not a problem too big in our lives that God cannot resolve. How can we be certain God will always keep his promises? 1) God is faithful, 2) God is not a liar, 3) God is not slow in keeping his promises, 4) God is able and just, and 5) his blessings upon his children bring him glory and, most importantly, his word confirms and reaffirms that he will!

There are ways we can be assured of his promises in our lives:

1. We must stay close to the Lord through the reading of his word.
2. Incorporate diligent prayers in our daily life (asking for his wisdom and a discerning spirit).
3. Surround ourselves with firm believers—Christlike confidantes and encouragers in everyday life.

We can all grow impatient and suffer mentally, emotionally, and spiritually when we feel God has not answered our prayers. We must remind ourselves of a key tactic the enemy thrives on, and that is leading us to believe our God has abandoned us or he will not answer our prayers, for he's the master of doubt and unbelief. But our situation can change when we stay close to the Lord and realize that he's in control and whatever he wills—"It is well with my soul." Our faith must be steadfast in Him alone—committed wholeheartedly, regardless.

God's word reminds us in 2 Pet 1:3, "By his divine power, God has given us everything we need for living a godly life. We have received all of this by coming to know him, the one who called us to himself by means of his marvelous glory and excellence." This is a perfect guide for us to follow where we can apply the knowledge of God's word in our lives—when it pertains to growth. Because His growth in us is the development of every area we need that reassures us—God has our best interest at heart.

When we seek His guidance or deliverance from a difficult situation in our life, God knows where we are. He has put us there or allowed it for his perfect purpose and plan. God will use trials to strengthen our patience and Christlike faith towards maturity and aim to be more like his Son.

That's a tough toll and a high calling, but his word promises he will never forsake us, and all things work together for the good *for those who love him and are called according to his purpose* (Rom 8:28). Sarah and Abraham's story is a great example. And always remember his faithfulness is unconditional. "If we are unfaithful, He remains faithful, for he cannot deny who he is" (2 Tim 2:13).

When we rest in God's promises and provisions, we can be confident that our lives *can depend on him and him alone—no matter what*. Psalm 23 reminds us the shepherd meets the sheep's every need: food, water, rest, safety, and direction. So, as believers, when we follow our *Shepherd and allow him to be Lord of our life*, we should always realize we have all we need. We will not lack the necessities of life, for he is our Provider and Sustainer!

"Don't worry about anything; instead, pray about everything. Tell God what you need and thank him for all he has done. Then you will experience God's peace, which exceeds anything we can understand. His peace will guard your hearts and minds as you live in Christ Jesus" (Phil 4:6–7). Believe this passage with all your heart, soul, mind, and strength!

CHAPTER 22

Developing Us

Sometime later, God tested Abraham's faith. "Abraham!" God called. "Yes," he replied. "Here I am." "Take your son, your only son—yes, Isaac, whom you love so much—and go to the land of Moriah. Go and sacrifice him as a burnt offering on one of the mountains, which I will show you." When they arrived at the place where God had told him to go, Abraham built an altar and arranged the wood on it. Then he tied his son, Isaac, and laid him on the altar on top of the wood. And Abraham picked up the knife to kill his son as a sacrifice. At that moment the angel of the LORD called to him from heaven, "Abraham! Abraham!" "Yes," Abraham replied. "Here I am!" "Don't lay a hand on the boy!" the angel said. "Do not hurt him in any way, for now I know that you truly fear God. You have not withheld from me even your son, your only son." Then Abraham looked up and saw a ram caught by its horns in a thicket. So, he took the ram and sacrificed it as a burnt offering in place of his son. (Gen 22:1–2, 9–13)

That morning, Abraham began one of the most extraordinary acts of obedience known to man—in one of the most symbolic stories in the Bible and literature. As God gave Abraham this command, not once did Abraham question God. He got up without delay or hesitation and started the journey. And when it came time to sacrifice his *"only son,"* the one he loved and long-awaited, the son of promise, he did not argue or dispute God's order—but was obedient to God's command.

In a beautiful statement from Spurgeon, *"That knife was cutting into his own heart all the while, yet he took it. Unbelief would have left the knife at* home, but *genuine faith takes it*."[1] What an unbelievable act of faith! Abraham did not leave the knife at home because his genuine faith in God took the knife knowing that he would sacrifice his son Isaac. All along, the knife was cutting into the depths of Abraham's heart, realizing he was going to take the life of his precious son.

Abraham's undeniable display of a faithful heart towards God through his willingness to give up his only son is incomparable. But here's the beautiful portrayal of this story: God displays his heart towards us in the same way by giving his *only begotten Son as the ultimate sacrifice for each one of us who believes (John 3:16)!*

God never intended for Isaac to die because the test was in the heart of Abraham's faith. Would he love his son more than God—or be obedient to God's command? It was to validate Abraham as the "father of all" with ultimate faith in God—and he passed the test.

When they reached their destination on the mountain, the sacrifice would continue. God would provide the substitute as a ram caught in a thicket behind Abraham. After the sacrifice, Abraham names the mountain "The Lord will provide." Then the Lord not only renews his promises to Abraham but emphasizes to him once more, swearing by himself. *Because of Abraham's obedience,* the Lord promises to bless Abraham, multiply his offspring, and give Abraham's offspring victory over their enemies (Gen 22:15-17).

Sometimes we need to be purified, tested, and validated to see where our genuine faith lies, which could come at a cost and hurt deeply. When God tests our faith, it's his way of developing our character to be more Christlike. It's deepening our capacity to deal with obedience more and more each step of our way throughout life. Obeying God can be difficult, for it may mean giving up something we want or love. Still, as genuine children of God, we should not expect it to be easy or come naturally. It's when we allow the power of his Holy Spirit to indwell in us and give us the strength and ability to endure and persevere. "Dear brothers and sisters, when troubles of any kind come your way, consider it an opportunity for great joy, for you know that when your faith is tested, your endurance has a chance to grow. So let it grow, for when your endurance is fully developed, you will be perfect and complete, needing nothing" (Jas 1:2-4).

Jesus commands us to obey (John 14:15) and always remember that godly obedience will lead us to acts of worship (Rom 12:1). It proves our love for the Lord and demonstrates our faith (such as the case with Abraham). We experience the blessings of holy living, and there's no greater blessing.

---

1. Spurgeon, "Spurgeon's Verse Expositions," Gen 22:6.

"Joyful are people of integrity, who follow the instructions of the LORD. Joyful are those who obey His laws and search for Him with all their hearts. They do not compromise with evil and walk only in His paths" (Ps 119:1–3). *A yearning spirit will always yield to the power of the Holy Spirit for more Christlike development in their daily life. Oh, how rewarding!*

> Now if you will obey me and keep my covenant, you will be my own special treasure from among all the peoples on earth; for all the earth belongs to me. (Exod 19:5)

CHAPTER 23

His Good Season

When Sarah was 127 years old, she died at Kiriath-arba (now called Hebron) in the land of Canaan. There Abraham mourned and wept for her. Then, leaving her body, he said to the Hittite elders, "Here I am, a stranger and a foreigner among you. Please sell me a piece of land so I can give my wife a proper burial." (Gen 23:1–4)

In the days of Abraham, proper burial was critical to a person's character and integrity; it showed respect and their steepness in rituals and traditions. Many would consider an improper burial a curse. One reason is that the idea of being left unburied and vulnerable to animals and birds of prey was shameful. It was especially desirable to be buried in one's native land and, if possible, with one's ancestors.

Mourning expresses deep sorrow for someone who has passed—and is a familiar theme throughout the Bible. Common ways to show mourning in biblical times included weeping (Ps 6:6) and crying loudly. But God limited Jewish expressions of mourning to keep them from copying the paganism of other nations.

In Eccl 3, God reminds us, "That to everything there's a season—a time for every purpose under Heaven," which includes life and death, mourning, and happiness. Through difficult times such as a loss of a close one—we all know it's hard and we don't always understand, but we should be content with what God is showing us in his word—because there lies his peace, comfort, and guidance. Solomon was the wisest man in the Bible, and through God's guidance, he gives us instructive insight on preparing for things to come in our lifetime.

Today, we live in a world of ongoing changes, difficult times, unexpected occurrences, and various conditions of human life. So many are beyond our control, but we know Who is in control. When a loved one dies, we mourn—but we do not grieve as the world does because we have an eternal hope that the world does not possess. First Thessalonians 4:13–18 reminds us that death is not the end for those who are in Jesus Christ—and our mourning is temporary. Mourning is not pleasant, but it will happen in our lifetime. However, those who have Jesus look forward to the day when "God will wipe away every tear" (Rev 7:17; 21:4). What a beautiful depiction of an unbelievable future reality—one with no more pain, mourning, or crying in eternity. We will be free from all our sufferings as we enjoy an everlasting unbroken fellowship with our Heavenly Father.

As humans, we must realize there are things beyond our control. God appoints each moment and time for all things, a mixture of joy and sorrow, pleasure and pain, peace and struggle, and life and death. Each season has its appropriate time in this cycle of life. Nothing stays the same, so we must learn to accept and adjust to God's way of controlling all of life's conditions.

Of course, some seasons are more difficult than others, and we may not understand what God is doing during those times. Still, we must humbly submit to the Lord's will and trust that he works out his good purpose and plan. "And we know that all things work together for good to them that love God, to them who are the called according to His purpose" (Rom 8:28). Even when we believe and recognize in the depths of our heart that God controls all things it still takes spiritual effort and diligence on our part.

There will be many times throughout our journey we need to humbly ask God to grant us his wisdom and understanding, and we must always be steadfast in our genuine faith (Jas 1:5–8). Suppose we ground ourselves in the depths of his word and let it fill our minds and hearts. In that case, the sovereign ways of God will become more apparent to each of us. And then we will rejoice in those things because we trust (wholeheartedly) that God has them in his Hands. And always be mindful of this—he has a perfect purpose and plan to give us a greater hope for tomorrow.

> God blesses those who mourn, for they will be comforted. (Matt 5:4)

CHAPTER 24

The Little Things

> One day Abraham said to his oldest servant, the man in charge of his household, "Take an oath by putting your hand under my thigh. Swear by the LORD, the God of heaven and earth, that you will not allow my son to marry one of these local Canaanite women. Go instead to my homeland, to my relatives, and find a wife there for my son Isaac." The servant asked, "But what if I can't find a young woman who is willing to travel so far from home? Should I then take Isaac there to live among your relatives in the land you came from?" "No!" Abraham responded. "Be careful never to take my son there. For the LORD, the God of heaven, who took me from my father's house and my native land, solemnly promised to give this land to my descendants. He will send his angel ahead of you, and he will see to it that you find a wife there for my son. If she is unwilling to come back with you, then you are free from this oath of mine. But under no circumstances are you to take my son there." So, the servant took an oath by putting his hand under the thigh of his master, Abraham. He swore to follow Abraham's instructions. (Gen 24:2–9)

Eliezer was not only a trusted servant of the patriarch Abraham, but he was a "senior servant," because he would have inherited Abraham's fortune if Ishmael and Isaac were not born. But in Gen 24, *his name is not mentioned as "Eliezer the trusted and senior servant"* . . . *he's noted as "the servant."* And the power of his commitment and loyalty illustrates a beautiful depiction of what our servanthood should look like as Christ followers of Jesus Christ.

As you read his appointed task in the first twenty-seven verses, you will see that Eliezer 1) listened to his master; 2) sought clarity; 3) heeded the call (he was a doer); 4) took an oath to fulfill the call; 5) humbly prayed for success, but showed kindness to his master; 6) "continued to pray" for a sign; and 7) praised and worshiped the Lord with thanks—not to him, but honor to his master. And lo and behold, God revealed everything to the servant before his eyes.

In this portrayal of a "genuine godly servant", we see a heart that displays an undeniable level of loyalty and faithfulness—*one that illustrates "quality" more so than quantity. Always remember this saying—many little things with quality will always supercede the "quantity" of many things with no value*—ouch!

God cares about the "little things" in our lives because he cares about us. After all, our lives comprise those "little things." Psalm 139:17–18 says, "How precious to me are your thoughts, O God! How vast is the sum of them, were I to count them, they would outnumber the grains of sand? When I am awake, I am still with you." And in Matt 25:21, "The master was full of praise. 'Well done, my good and faithful servant. You have been faithful in handling this small amount, so now I will give you many more responsibilities. Let's celebrate together!'"

I read this in an article not too long ago. "Rank is given to enable you to better serve those above and below you. It is not given for you to practice your idiosyncrasies. What a powerful statement for those who allow their eccentric, quirky, and selfish behaviors to impede on being a reliable, trusted, and loyal servant. We cannot let the little petty things get ahead of our proper place of service for the Lord!

A trusted servant does not care about their name being broadcasted or in bright lights. They don't want the credit or glory, for they are "focused on the quality of the task given to them by their master." They have swallowed pride and now display humility, grace, and "selflessness" in their actions. In it all—they're doing it for God's glory! No matter how tiny it may be!

> Don't be selfish; don't try to impress others. Be humble, thinking of others as better than yourselves. Don't look out only for your interests, but take an interest in others, too. (Phil 2:3–4)

CHAPTER 25

God's Ways

> Isaac pleaded with the LORD on behalf of his wife, because she was unable to have children. The LORD answered Isaac's prayer, and Rebekah became pregnant with twins. But the two children struggled with each other in her womb. So, she went to ask the LORD about it. "Why is this happening to me?" she asked. And the LORD told her, "The sons in your womb will become two nations. From the very beginning, the two nations will be rivals. One nation will be stronger than the other; and your older son will serve your younger son." (Gen 25:21-23)

An answered prayer—twenty years after Isaac and Rebekah were first married (Gen 25:20, 26). Their faith and persistence in prayer may have been tested, but it invited them to grow through this experience for many years.

The struggle that seemed to take place in Rebekah's womb made her seek God because he gave her a prophecy during her pregnancy. She noticed that the twins were struggling against one another in her womb, and she asked the Lord why they were fighting. The Lord told her that two nations were in her womb and those nations would be at odds with one another (Gen 25:22-23), and this prophecy came true.

God's choice between Jacob and Esau, regarding which one would be the heir of God's covenant of salvation, was all part of God's divine plan. However, it seemed to make less sense to man. Paul wrote that God's choice was not based on the performance of Jacob or Esau—it was made when they were not even born and had not done any good or evil (Rom 9:11).

God is above and beyond our ability to comprehend his ways. But God has not left us ignorant about himself because he has revealed himself to us through his word and the power of his Spirit. If not, we would not know or understand his divine nature. Therefore, we can know God and learn how to be reconciled to him through his Son—and live according to his will, purpose, and plan. Even though God is infinite, he allows us to tap into his divine wisdom and glimpse his sovereign ways—when we have absolute faith in him (Jas 1:5–8).

Today, we recognize God's powerful ways when he intervenes in our lives through healing, delivering us from difficult circumstances, and seeing his gracious provisions. And when he meets our needs, we are always pleased. But here's the gut punch—*we must be pleased with all his ways*. Why? Because he may choose to withhold an unanswered prayer for an unspecified amount of time to deepen our faith, and increase our wisdom and knowledge, which would allow us to mature and grow closer to him.

God chooses according to his divine wisdom, love, and goodness. We may not understand God's reasons for choosing, which are reasons he alone knows and answers to, but God's choices are not random. Always remember his word in Isa 55:8–9 "My thoughts are nothing like your thoughts," says the Lord. "And my ways are far beyond anything you could imagine. For just as the heavens are higher than the earth, my ways are higher than yours and my thoughts higher than yours."

The best way to understand God is through an unbelievable and close relationship with his Son—Jesus Christ, and giving way to the power of his indwelling Spirit. Through him, we pursue right living and yield to all his sovereign ways in our daily life. We cling to his word, for they provide us with his righteous ways of living. And now, just as you accepted Christ Jesus as your Lord, you must continue to follow him. Let your roots grow down into him, and let your lives be built on him. Then your faith will grow strong in the truth you were taught, and you will overflow with thankfulness. Don't let anyone capture you with empty philosophies and high-sounding nonsense that come from human thinking and from the spiritual powers of this world, rather than from Christ. For in Christ lives all the fullness of God in a human body. So, you also are complete through your union with Christ, who is the head over every ruler and authority (Col 2:6–10).

As followers of Jesus Christ when we're grounded and rooted in the richness and fullness of his word—then his ways are evident in our lives mentally, emotionally, physically, and most importantly—spiritually. When our lives are submissive to him, the world sees Who is Lord of our life. Through our growing process, we're allowing him to lead, build, and strengthen us in all his ways. And then we will have a better understanding of what he's doing—and why He's doing it!!

> I will show mercy to anyone I choose and compassion to anyone
> I choose. (Rom 9:15)

WEEK 6

Godly Path

Gen 26–30

As we progress in week 6, our daily steps with the Lord become more evident as we adhere to God's path of righteousness. We're keener in noticing those opportunities where we can share His good news because of our growth, and we don't wait—we seize it. Christlike integrity shows up within us with more clarity, and He gives us more insight into areas of patience and endurance. A godly path means a way of living. Our sights are on His path that presses forward and does not sway from side to side or set us back.

A believer on a Godly path is striving to live a holy life, a natural outgrowth of someone in God's grace because they're filled with his Spirit. But we also realize we cannot give up when we mess up, for they remember there's no condemnation for those in Christ Jesus. So even when we're at a crossroads, that discerning spirit leads us down the right path.

It is easy to identify people who walk with God because their lives possess a stark contrast with the world around them. They produce the fruit of the Spirit (Gal 5:22–23) rather than the vices of fleshly desire (Gal 5:19–21). In Acts 4:13, Peter and John had been arrested for preaching and were brought before the leading authorities. "It amazed the members of the council when they saw the boldness of Peter and John, for they could see that they were ordinary men with no special training in the Scriptures. They also recognized them as men who had been with Jesus." When we walk with God daily, the world cannot help but recognize that clear indicator of his presence in our life! Despite our imperfections and lack of knowledge in some areas—the Truth is full of light and removes all darkness. Is the world amazed by your Christlikeness?

CHAPTER 26

Our Opportunity

> One day King Abimelech came from Gerar with his adviser, Ahuzzath, and also Phicol, his army commander. "Why have you come here?" Isaac asked. "You obviously hate me, since you kicked me off your land." They replied, "We can plainly see that the Lord is with you. So, we want to enter into a sworn treaty with you. Let's make a covenant. Swear that you will not harm us, just as we have never troubled you. We have always treated you well, and we sent you away from us in peace. And now look how the Lord has blessed you!" (Gen 26:26–29)

Earlier in this chapter, we identified when Isaac followed in the same footsteps as his father, Abraham, for he also deceived King Abimelech. But later, after Abimelech witnessed the prosperity Isaac was gaining off his land, he told Isaac to leave Gerar (for Isaac had the favor of God upon him). What a powerful twist in this passage. It starts with Isaac telling Abimelech and his advisers that this is not a friendly visit. You would sense in this opening line tragedy is coming. But it was an open door of celebration. Abimelech wanted a covenant with Isaac because he witnessed God's blessings upon him. Here, we must take note of the tremendous practical wisdom of Isaac's actions; he didn't respond to evil with more evil—he sought God's provision! After a feast marking their covenant of peace, Abimelech departed from Isaac.

When the world recognizes the influence of God in our life, and they're attracted to us even if they are our enemies, that is an excellent opportunity for us to plant seeds and reach out to them with God's love—and share the good news. God's word tells us that love originates in God (1 Cor 13:4–8)! Of all God's greatest gifts are faith, hope, and love, and "the greatest is love."

The Bible tells us in John 3:16 that God was motivated by love to save the world. Also, in 1 John 4:9, God's word reminds us that his love is best seen in the sacrifice of Christ on our behalf. God's love does not require us to be "worthy" to receive it; his love is truly kind, merciful, and gracious. God demonstrates his love for us in this: "While we were still sinners, Christ died for us" (Rom 5:8). And the Bible reminds us *that nothing can separate the believer from the love of God in Christ* (Rom 8:38–39). This passage effectively shows God's wonderful provision for all his children who are in Christ.

Those who recognize God's provisions in their life realize this is the type of love we should instill in the very heart of our being. Because that kind of love in and through us will open the door to all opportunities where we can witness to others, share our testimony, help those in need, serve where we can, and be the Christlike example God intended.

God's word reminds us in Col 3:14, "Above all, clothe yourselves with love, which binds us all together in perfect harmony." If these words are our marching orders, there should be no gap between anyone regarding us exemplifying God's unconditional love. The more we know God's will through His word, the more we possess that closeness with his Spirit. That's when our growth and maturity elevate, and we will seize those opportunities for love and service.

When a circumstance arises that makes it possible for us to capture a splitting moment of serving our Lord, it's then when our yielding to the power of his Spirit comes to fruition and is pleasing to Him. Those who know his will and continuously grow will never live in a way that's not pleasing to our Lord. Instead, they will cooperate with God according to his desires and pursue those opportunities in life to serve him in glorious ways. Every precious moment of service matters in his eyes, no matter how big or small.

"So let's not get tired of doing what is good. At just the right time, we will reap a harvest of blessing if we don't give up. Therefore, whenever we have the opportunity, we should do good to everyone—especially to those in the family of faith" (Gal 6:9–10).

> Finally, brothers, rejoice. Aim for restoration, comfort one another, agree with one another, live in peace; and the God of love and peace will be with you. (2 Cor 13:11)

CHAPTER 27

Genuine Honesty

> But Rebekah overheard what Isaac had said to his son Esau. So, when Esau left to hunt for the wild game, she said to her son Jacob, "Listen. I overheard your father say to Esau, 'Bring me some wild game and prepare me a delicious meal. Then I will bless you in the Lord's presence before I die.' Now, my son, listen to me. Do exactly as I tell you. Go out to the flocks and bring me two fine young goats. I'll use them to prepare your father's favorite dish. Then take the food to your father so he can eat it and bless you before he dies." (Gen 27:5-10).

God had already told Rebekah that Jacob would become the heir—the leader. But she still went into panic mode and took matters into her own hands. The bottom line is that she resorted to doing the *wrong thing, even after God had told her what would happen.*

Rebekah knew she could concoct a tasteful dish equal to Esau. It doesn't seem at this moment that Jacob is all that concerned about Rebekah's deceitful act; he is only worried about being caught. But, wrong motives will keep compounding to more and more trouble ahead, for Jacob would soon pay a considerable price—a prolonged and delayed gratification, which can eat away at your spirit and soul.

When we're not in line with God—and we know something doesn't feel right—do we ever feel so concerned or convicted about getting caught in the act? If not, we're probably in a position where there's no presence of honesty or integrity. So, our fear of doing wrong or getting caught should be a telltale sign we must repent and go the other route.

We live in a world full of lies, and deceit comes from many sources. There are lying spirits who lead us astray (1 Tim 4:1); there are "evildoers and impostors" looking for ways to trick us (2 Tim 3:13), and we have ourselves to deal with, as well. Self-deception is common in our fallen world because our hearts are so deceitful—so much so we can easily fool ourselves (Jer 17:9).

Remembering the word of God, doing the word of God, and continuing in the word of God changes character and self-deception. Like a mirror, His word will always show us the truth. Remember what God's word tells us in John 14:6—Christ is the Way, Truth, and Life. So, if Christ is Truth, lying is moving away from Christ, which is the opposite direction in life! But, on the other hand, being honest is following in God's footsteps every step of our Christian life. Why? Because God cannot lie (Titus 1:2), and that should be our lifelong example.

To be honest means we're always sincere, truthful, and without deceit. And that establishes a clear conscience with a peace of mind. It helps maintain self-respect and Christlike integrity that flows from one to another. And what a sweet sense of aroma for our Lord to see this quality in our daily life.

When we are honest, we're building a Christlike character that will enable us to be of excellent service to God and others. As a result, the Lord will trust us because we're now walking in a manner that's worthy of our calling (Eph 4:1). This lifestyle enables us to approach him because it would be impossible to approach our Father's throne of mercy, love, and grace when our motives and desires are not in line with his actual characteristics.

Along with honesty is its hand-in-hand partner—integrity, which means thinking and doing what is always right, no matter the consequences. When we have integrity, we will live by our Christian standards and beliefs—*even when no one is watching us.* When we choose to live this type of life, it becomes habitual—like second nature. Then our spiritual thoughts and behaviors will always be in harmony and in tune with the ways of our Lord, and that's indisputable truth and a life worth living!

> You have been deceived by your own pride because you live in a rock fortress and make your home high in the mountains." Who can ever reach us way up here?" you ask boastfully. (Obad 3:1)

CHAPTER 28

God's Clarity

Meanwhile, Jacob left Beersheba and traveled toward Haran. At sundown he arrived at a good place to set up camp and stopped there for the night. *Jacob found a stone to rest his head against and lay down to sleep.* As he slept, he dreamed of a stairway that reached from the earth up to heaven. And he saw the angels of God going up and down the stairway. At the top of the stairway stood the Lord, and he said, "I am the Lord, the God of your grandfather Abraham, and the God of your father, Isaac. The ground you are lying on belongs to you. I am giving it to you and your descendants. Your descendants will be as numerous as the dust of the earth! They will spread out in all directions—to the west and the east, to the north and the south. And all the families of the earth will be blessed through you and your descendants. What's more, I am with you, and I will protect you wherever you go. One day I will bring you back to this land. I will not leave you until I have finished giving you everything, I have promised you." (Gen 28:12–15)[1]

In this passage, we see a beautiful symbol of resting our minds on the Rock of our Salvation. Jacob had a significant dream in this desolate wilderness and even used a stone for a pillow. When Jacob got up early the next morning, he took the very stone he used to rest his head upon and dedicated it to the Lord. I can only imagine the overwhelming emotions in Jacob at this moment—the fear, the loneliness, the isolation, the excitement, and the anticipation; this was an important time in Jacob's life.

In Jacob's dream, there was no access to heaven. However, Jacob knew God was closer than he ever thought because at this moment, there was real

1. My emphasis.

access and interaction with the Almighty One. Jacob did not doubt the great God who appeared to Abraham and Isaac because this same God met Jacob personally. It was a life-changing experience for Jacob. For God says, "I will give the land on which you lie to you and your descendants."

These words were comforting for Jacob at this critical crossroad in his life, and this was the game-changer because—the same promise offered to Abraham and Isaac was offered to Jacob. And although Jacob was the grandson of the great Patriarch Abraham—that was not enough because Jacob would be required to establish his own personal relationship with God!

The clarity of God, also called God's perspicuity, is explained by theologian Wayne Grudem to mean "that the Bible is written in such a way that its teachings can be understood by all who will read it—seek God's help and being willing to follow it."

Our greatest life-changing experience happens when we confess, accept, believe, and know the person of Jesus Christ as our Savior and we have his indwelling Spirit then working within us. And then, as his faithful students, clarity reveals to us the greatest blessing of all: Jesus Christ is alive and in our midst, right now, at work. And we can join his work, learning from him and loving the people around us in his name.

The Bible is God's revelation of himself and his purposes throughout history, teaching us about our Savior throughout scripture. God has revealed himself to us with the most clarity in the person of his only Son—Jesus Christ. He is the living, breathing, flesh-and-blood human presentation of God.

God reminds us in Eccl 3:11 that within the heart of every person, God has planted a longing to know him. From Genesis to Revelation, Scripture is God's revelation of himself and all his Ways for us all to read, understand, and apply to our daily life.

Many people can acknowledge the fact that there is a God. But God wants us to know him personally through His Son and spend all eternity in close fellowship with him. So then, when you're in the family of God through Christ, there's no more cloudiness and confusion—your destiny is crystal clear.

> They know the truth about God because he has made it obvious to them. (Rom 1:19)

CHAPTER 29

Diligent Endurance

Since Jacob was in love with Rachel, he told her father, "I'll work for you for seven years if you'll give me Rachel, your younger daughter, as my wife." "Agreed!" Laban replied. "I'd rather give her to you than to anyone else. Stay and work with me." So, Jacob worked seven years to pay for Rachel. But his love for her was so strong that it seemed to him but a few days. Finally, the time came for him to marry her. "I have fulfilled my agreement," Jacob said to Laban. "Now give me my wife so I can sleep with her." So, Laban invited everyone in the neighborhood and prepared a wedding feast. But that night, when it was dark, Laban took Leah to Jacob, and he slept with her. (Laban had given Leah a servant, Zilpah, to be her maid.) But when Jacob woke up in the morning—it was Leah! "What have you done to me?" Jacob raged at Laban. "I worked seven years for Rachel! Why have you tricked me?" "It's not our custom here to marry off a younger daughter ahead of the firstborn," Laban replied. "But wait until the bridal week is over; then we'll give you Rachel, too—provided you promise to work another seven years for me." So, Jacob agreed to work seven more years. A week after Jacob had married Leah, Laban gave him Rachel, too. (Gen 29:18–28)

Laban (Jacob's uncle) manipulated others for his own benefit—he used his daughters, was a deceiver, liar, self-ambitious, and never admitted his wrongdoings. I am pretty sure we've seen a Laban in our lifetime. Always remember, "For we are not fighting against flesh-and-blood enemies, but against evil rulers and authorities of the unseen world, against mighty powers in this dark world, and against evil spirits in the heavenly places" (Eph 6:12).

I cannot imagine how Jacob felt working seven years for Laban, thinking he would wed one of Laban's daughters (Rachel—his first love) but tricked into marrying Rachel's sister (Leah). He could have thrown in the towel after those first seven years and never married Rachel, which would have been enormous—for she would be the mother of Joseph and Benjamin!

However, Jacob had such an unbelievable aspiration, passion, and desire to marry Rachel (whom he loved more) that he would commit to working another seven years for Laban. God's plan will always come to fruition—even when confronted with barriers—because he will provide us with undeniable endurance when our motives and desires align with his plan.

Do you ever feel like giving up, throwing in the towel, and even wondering if God is on your side? But your desire for that one thing is so great and intense you will go to all extremes. You're not giving up—you will endure and persevere no matter what!

But unfortunately, as you proceed diligently and wholeheartedly, the enemy is still putting up barriers and distractions—again and again. He will go to all extremes to prevent our plan from success. And, it may seem that a close one is distracting and preventing us from a God-driven purpose.

However, you know through fervent prayer and counseling that this path you're on is part of God's plan. Even though the enemy tries his best to prevent your action plan from success, you press on, for you know this powerful scripture "If God is for you, who can be against you?" (Rom 8:31)

Unfortunately, close ones can take advantage of us and others, leading us to make poor decisions and to a series of problems. But always remember God handles unfair treatment in his timing. Therefore, we should always pray for his wisdom, guidance, grace, mercy, patience, and discerning spirit when dealing with matters involving others close to us.

And again, God reminds us in Col 3:12-14, "Since God chose you to be the holy people he loves, you must clothe yourselves with tenderhearted mercy, kindness, humility, gentleness, and patience. Make allowance for each other's faults and forgive anyone who offends you." Remember, the Lord forgave you, so you must forgive others. But, above all, clothe yourselves with love, which binds us all together in perfect harmony."

And when you're in harmony with the Lord—you're in sync with him, you are in a continued single motion with the One who will see you through—because endurance will pay dividends!

> So be strong and courageous, all you who put your hope in the Lord! (Ps 31:24)

CHAPTER 30

Wait!

> When Rachel saw that she wasn't having any children for Jacob, she became jealous of her sister. She pleaded with Jacob, "Give me children, or I'll die!" Then Jacob became furious with Rachel. "Am I God?" he asked. "He's the one who has kept you from having children!" Then Rachel told him, "Take my maid, Bilhah, and sleep with her. She will bear children for me, and through her I can have a family, too." (Gen 30:1–3)

The great patriarchs, Abraham, Isaac, and Jacob, all had wives who had difficulty conceiving children. Abraham and Jacob chose to have children through their wives' servants, while Isaac decided to pray to God, and eventually, after twenty years of prayer, God answered. In Isaac's tale, we see a valuable lesson in waiting on God (even though it may take years) because, in Abraham and Jacob's storyline, there were some bitter and sad consequences. But even amidst the tension between Rachel and her sister, Jacob saw the hand of God with his response above—even though it came across as short and cruel.

In it all—God wants us to trust him when all seems bleak. And we must always practice patience and let God act in his timing to prevent heartaches and pain. The great example for us in God's word is this—in time, he would bless Rachel with two most prominent sons—Joseph and Benjamin.

Waiting on God can be very difficult (when we're in the flesh)—sometimes impossible. Why? We want things to happen in our own timing. But God doesn't operate on our schedule, and we're disappointed when it does not happen according to our plan.

Waiting on God is never easy, *but we wait in the knowledge that God knows our situation, he cares for our needs, and he is good to the end.* "Hope deferred makes the heart sick, but a longing fulfilled is a tree of life" (Prov 13:12).

There is a crucial point in waiting on God! It is a good thing because he is preparing us for what is on the other side, and it will reveal his faithfulness—because he is faithful in *all circumstances*. God's word reminds us of this powerful passage in Isa 40:31: "But those who trust in the Lord will find new strength. They will soar high on wings like eagles. They will run and not grow weary. They will walk and not faint." One of the greatest lessons we can learn when waiting on God is not only Christlike patience but humility because it's the quality of showing respect to others. But most importantly to our Lord—waiting on his timing!

- *Willing*—2 Cor 8:12, "For if the readiness is there, it is acceptable according to what a person has, not according to what he does not have."
- *Accepting*—1 Thess 5:18, "Be thankful in all circumstances, for this is God's will for you who belong to Christ Jesus."
- *Imitating*—1 Cor 11:1, "And you should imitate me, just as I imitate Christ."
- *Trusting*—Prov 3:5-6 (ESV), "Trust in the Lord with all your heart, and do not lean on your own understanding."

> Wait patiently for the Lord. Be brave and courageous. Yes, wait patiently for the Lord. (Ps 27:14)

WEEK 7

Chosen to Glorify

Gen 31–35

In week 7 (chapters 31–35), we will see how a child of God is chosen to glorify the Lord in ways that the ordinary man cannot. When we think of glorifying someone, we elevate them with honor and admiration; we put them on a pedestal. We see their qualities as something we may envy or possess like an athlete, political leader, singer, or actor. Why do we put these people at such a higher level of respect and prestige? In this world, we even glamorize the mortal ones. We often glorify man, but are too often disappointed by their selfish desires. It's as if we've exchanged the glory of the incorruptible and immortal God for the credit of the corruptible and mortal man (Rom 1:22–23).

God's glory is expressed to us in the incarnation of Jesus Christ—his Son. When Christ's life radiates through us that is how we can glorify God. Christ is the radiance of the glory of God and the exact imprint of his nature. He's our perfect example to follow as a living testimony that should be on display every day of our life. It does not mean we will reach perfection. Still, in our sanctified life, it is the outward expression of the inward salvation we have received by faith in what Christ did on the cross. His display of love, mercy, and grace on the cross is the life we're to portray daily. *Dead to self and alive in him, it should be so profound nothing can hide it.*

To be sanctified means that God's word has influenced us. It is "through the word" that God cleanses us and makes us holy (Eph 5:26). We're set apart for something unique, and that's glorifying him in everything we say and do.

CHAPTER 31

Don't Compare

> But Jacob soon learned that Laban's sons were grumbling about him. "Jacob has robbed our father of everything!" they said. "He has gained all his wealth at our father's expense." And Jacob began to notice a change in Laban's attitude toward him. Then the Lord said to Jacob, "Return to the land of your father and grandfather and to your relatives there, and I will be with you. (Gen 31:1-3)

The problem wasn't that Jacob stole anything—the problem was Laban's sons were full of envy and jealousy! And when these two evils are at work, they will distort the truth. Jacob had taken nothing of Laban's, but it shows us when these types of unrighteous vices are enforced they can lead to discord and division.

Although Laban mistreated Jacob, God still increased Jacob's prosperity. What a beautiful picture illustrating God's power is not limited because of someone else's evilness or fair play. Despite all the unfairness Jacob endured, he thrived because of God's favor!

We must remember *all sin separates us from God*, which means we should take it seriously I am as guilty in this area as the next, and I'm talking about the sin of comparison. It's so rooted in our lives because of our sinful nature. When I stop to think about it, I am guilty of comparison, envy, and jealousy, which shows me how weak my flesh is.

Too often in life, when comparing our possessions or financial status to others, we may give envy and jealousy a foothold—and that's what the enemy wants. We can avoid it by rejoicing in the blessings and successes others have received from God. When we take the *focus off us* and think about the *well-being of others—with pure motives*, it's then we are more in tune with God's love and care for all.

Envy is no minor sin, for it put Jesus on the cross, "He knew very well that the religious leaders had arrested Jesus out of envy" (Matt 27:18). But here's the big takeaway—God wants to deliver us from envy. In Titus 3, God's word reminds us as Christians; we move from these vices of sin to one that the Holy Spirit leads. We progress in righteous living—doing what is good. "Once we, too, were foolish and disobedient. We were misled and became slaves to many lusts and pleasures. Our lives were full of evil and envy, and we hated each other" (Titus 3:3).

We should root our daily measuring stick in the nine elements of the Fruit of the Spirit: love, joy, peace, patience, goodness, kindness, gentleness, faithfulness, and self-control (Gal 5:22–23). Still, way too often, we allow the enemy to creep into our minds and *"compare ourselves to others"* as a measuring stick in today's world.

When we assess our worth compared to other people's success and victories, it can beat us emotionally and, most importantly, rob our spiritual joy. Instead, our daily scale should be on how our Lord sees us, not anyone else. How God sees us unconditionally through his eyes can bring spiritual peace to our everyday life—*and a joy that's immeasurable and incomparable!*

> A peaceful heart leads to a healthy body; jealousy is like cancer in the bones. (Prov 14:30)

CHAPTER 32

Diligently Prepare

Then Jacob prayed, "O God of my grandfather Abraham, and God of my father, Isaac—O Lord, you told me, 'Return to your own land and to your relatives.' And you promised me, 'I will treat you kindly.' I am not worthy of all the unfailing love and faithfulness you have shown to me, your servant. When I left home and crossed the Jordan River, I owned nothing except a walking stick. Now my household fills two large camps! O Lord, please rescue me from the hand of my brother, Esau. I am afraid that he is coming to attack me, along with my wives and children. But you promised me, 'I will surely treat you kindly, and I will multiply your descendants until they become as numerous as the sands along the seashore—too many to count.'" (Gen 32:9-12)

It has been twenty years since Jacob last saw his furious brother Esau. And I am pretty sure Jacob was not looking forward to his upcoming meeting. If you recall, the last time they saw each other, Esau was angry and ready to kill his brother. He vowed to kill Jacob as soon as their father, Isaac, died. I cannot fathom the fear quivering through Jacob's body, soul, and spirit.

Jacob heard from his messengers that Esau was on his way with 400 men. So, to counter his dreadful fears, he was hoping to buy Esau's favor by sending him gifts. Can you imagine this unpleasant emotion stirring within Jacob? His flesh was controlling his thoughts and actions, but here's the turning point. His genuine prayer to the Lord would offset it all. *Below is a powerful comment from Spurgeon relating to the power of prayer.* The groans and tears of humble petitioners are as truly acceptable as the continual "Holy, holy, holy," of the Cherubim and Seraphim; for in their very essence all truthful confessions of personal fault are but a homage paid to the infinite perfections of the Lord of hosts.[1]

What good came out of Jacob's fear? It led him to prayer—to review his life, and seek a suitable promise from God. After first reacting in fear and unbelief, Jacob did the right thing—he went to the Lord with a solid prayer. It was a prayer of humility, full of faith, full of thanksgiving, and in line with God's way. Jacob remembered God's promises and held onto that "hope" in his prayer. Through this prayer, he was reminded our faithful God always keeps his promises.

We may be unable to keep people from speaking badly about us or treating us unfairly. Still, on the other hand, we cannot continue to give people ammunition to shoot our way. If we're diligently preparing and developing our Christlike values and yielding to the Holy Spirit, the accusations from our enemy will be empty. "Teach the truth so that your teaching can't be criticized. Then those who oppose us will be ashamed and have nothing bad to say about us" (Titus 2:8).

Living out his truth in our daily life demonstrates our Christlike diligence in how we prepare and develop a life more like Jesus. An essential part of our Christian walk when dealing with others is learning how Christ lived, behaved, and responded to people.

Suppose we're persistent in our efforts to develop Christlike attributes. In that case, it will enable us to be better prepared to serve God and others throughout our journey in life. This development stage is vital in portraying and conveying Christlikeness in our approach to others. Therefore, it should be our daily prerequisite!

> May the God of hope fill you with all joy and peace in believing so that by the power of the Holy Spirit, you may abound in hope. (Rom 15:13)

---

1. Spurgeon, "Power of Prayer," para. 4.

CHAPTER 33

A Past Made Right

> Then Jacob looked up and saw Esau coming with his 400 men. So, he divided the children among Leah, Rachel, and his two servant wives. He put the servant wives and their children at the front, Leah, and her children next, and Rachel and Joseph last. Then Jacob went on ahead. As he approached his brother, he bowed to the ground seven times before him. Then Esau ran to meet him and embraced him, threw his arms around his neck, and kissed him. And they both wept. (Gen 33:1–4)

This wonderful story continues from yesterday's lesson. Now we will see the power of Jacob's development come to fruition—and the benefits of how diligent preparation can make things right. When there's an impending clash, only when God is at the center point of the plan can healing have a chance!

The beauty of this story is that when the two brothers met, "Esau ran" to Jacob, embraced him affectionately, and kissed him. I am sure this is not what Jacob expected, but Esau's *change of heart superseded any past wrongdoings*. Jacob's prayer undoubtedly gave him discernment in his approach—for he bowed seven times and had the right choice of words. After all, Scripture tells us in Jacob's preparation, he hoped Esau would be friendly to them. Fervent and diligent prayers to our Loving Father will bring his healing Hands!

When the Lord leads us to heal pain from a past relationship, it can be spiritually, emotionally, and mentally challenging. Whether it was betrayal, deception, or something much deeper, God always provides us with the tools to handle any situation. The key is prayer, seeking his wisdom and guidance from his word, and always heed the direction of the Holy Spirit.

We must keep hurtful experiences from moving into our souls and creating an ill spirit.

The book of wisdom from the Bible says, "Guard your heart above all else, for it determines the course of your life" (Prov 4:23). We guard our hearts by carefully choosing our thoughts, feelings, attitudes, and actions.

Giving up bitterness takes Christlike grace and humility—"God opposes the proud but gives grace to the humble" (Jas 4:6; Prov 3:34). It takes a forgiving attitude (Eph 4:32; Col 3:13) with no slight inkling of revenge (Rom 12:19)—like it never happened! But it takes the power of the Holy Spirit working in and through us (Eph 3:16).

When we bring a matter to our loving Father's throne, it should be with the right heart. When we pursue the knowledge of the Lord, he will bless it, but it must be with pure motives. God's word tells us in Eph 4:2–3, "Always be humble and gentle. Be patient, making allowance for each other's faults because of your love. Make every effort to keep yourselves united in the Spirit, binding yourselves together with peace."

We must never forget—when we're attempting to make things right—we're Christ's representatives. It is always helpful and fruitful - when dealing with a deep issue or problem from the past, if the other party consistently sees Christ in our daily words and deeds. We must always be the model of Christlikeness and in line with his righteousness to make things right!

> Dear brothers and sisters, if another believer is overcome by some sin, you who are godly should gently and humbly help that person back onto the right path. And be careful not to fall into the same temptation yourself. (Gal 6:1)

CHAPTER 34

God Sees All

> One day Dinah, the daughter of Jacob and Leah, went to visit some of the young women who lived in the area. But when the local prince, Shechem son of Hamor the Hivite, saw Dinah, he seized her and raped her. But then he fell in love with her, and he tried to win her affection with tender words. He said to his father, Hamor, "Get me this young girl. I want to marry her." (Gen 34:1–4)

We could note chapter 34 as one of Genesis's most disgraceful and painful incidents. A horrible offense was committed against Dinah, but the reaction by her brothers was worse than the crime. Hamor and Shechem probably thought of themselves as generous in their approach and manner of negotiating the marriage arrangement. Still, they insulted Dinah and her family even more with a *"just name your price" attitude*. They acted as if money and marriage could make her disgrace go away. Shechem was attracted to Dinah, but it was not genuine love, and Shechem and Hamor *downplayed this one act as some small thing*.[1]

But the effect on all sides is sad, for even in Jacob's anger against his sons, he was only concerned about himself and what could happen to their family. Jacob would not forget what his two sons did. When he prophesied over his twelve sons before he died, he said that Simeon and Levi's "instruments of cruelty are in their dwelling place" (Gen 49:5–7). He saw them for who they were but rebuked them too late. This one incident had an incredible impact and effect on all the families involved. One sin can creep in and obliterate all parties involved.

---

1. See David Guzik's commentary on this chapter, esp. topic A3c: https://enduringword.com/bible-commentary/genesis-34.

So many believe our Almighty God is so "loving" that he will overlook those minor faults and little nasty speech and behaviors in our life. Little white lies, cheating on anything, hiding little secrets and behind-the-wall sins. "These are so minute! Indeed, my loving God will not hold these against me", we say in our finite minds! The problem is that sin is sin, big or small, and separates us from the will of God!

Although God loves us, God is a Holy God—who cannot partake in evil. Holiness is complete and total devotion to God and his ways, period! Any type of evilness is nowhere including in his portfolio. Habakkuk describes God this way: "But you are pure and cannot stand the sight of evil. Will you wink at their treachery?" (Hab 1:13).

The Bible describes those who choose to indulge in sin as being darkened in their understanding and separated from the life of God because of the ignorance that is in them due to the hardening of their hearts. That is: *S*tubbornness-*I*gnoring-*N*eglecting God's holiness in their daily life.

When someone continues to live in their sin, they have given over to their sensual desires to indulge in every kind of impurity, with a continual lust for more and more (Eph 4:18–19). *One consequence of habitual sin is—more sin.* A great comment I read is that when "there's an insatiable 'lust for more,' attended by a dulling of the conscience, [it leads to our] blindness to [His] spiritual truth (1 Corinthians 2:14)."[2]

The consequence of suppressing the Truth is that God gives the sinner over to "the sinful desires of their hearts," "shameful lusts," and "a depraved mind," as Rom 1 beautifully notes. The only answer to this is to repent and believe the good news of Jesus Christ (Mark 1:15)! There should be no room for evil behavior in our life—big or small that could separate us from our Almighty and Holy God.

> For the wages of sin is death, but the free gift of God is eternal life through Christ Jesus our Lord. (Rom 6:23)

---

2. "What Are the Consequences," para. 5.

CHAPTER 35

Set Apart

> Then God said to Jacob, "Get ready and move to Bethel and settle there. Build an altar there to the God who appeared to you when you fled from your brother, Esau." So, Jacob told everyone in his household, "Get rid of all your pagan idols, purify yourselves, and put on clean clothing. We are now going to Bethel, where I will build an altar to the God who answered my prayers when I was in distress. He has been with me wherever I have gone." (Gen 35:1–3)

When God spoke, Jacob did not hesitate. Jacob told his household to get rid of all their idols because he knew that if they didn't—it could ruin their faith. I love this passage because God said nothing to Jacob about the idols—he simply told Jacob to get ready and move to Bethel and build an altar to the God who appeared to you. How did Jacob know to tell his family to get rid of their idols and purify themselves?

Because as Jacob grew closer to God, he clearly understood the expectations of a Holy God when presenting themselves at the altar. Anything considered pagan idols, even good luck charms, earrings, or any idolatry used to ward off evil, had to be removed from their life. They had to separate themselves from anything considered "not holy" because, in God's eyes, "the only cure for worldliness is to separate ourselves from it"!

Many Christians recognize that some pagan ideas and practices have infiltrated the Christian church. Sadly, the early Christians re-established much of what Jesus Christ abolished by His death and resurrection. Jesus' sacrifice fulfilled God's requirements, ending the need for any further sacrifices (Hebrews 7:27; 10:10; 1 Peter 3:18). The early church, due to pagan influences, warped the celebration of the Lord's Supper into a re-sacrifice / re-offering of Christ's once-for-all sacrifice. Jesus' perfect sacrifice abolished the need of a formal priesthood (Hebrews 10:12-14), creating instead a "kingdom of priests" (Revelation 1:6; 5:10). The early church, again influenced by paganism, re-established a priesthood that added a barrier between the "ordinary" believer and God (1 Timothy 2:5; Hebrews 9:15). . . .

Most Christians wholeheartedly agree that beliefs / practices such as these need to be rejected and the biblical truth upheld [in the foundation of the church, within the body of all believers and taught by the leaders.][1]

The key to avoiding "pagan Christianity" is comparing every belief and practice with Scripture and removing anything that contradicts what the Bible prescribes for the church. When we're rooted in the Truth of his word and its teachings it will lead to our daily growth and a discerning spirit that will know "what is or is not" in unity with the Spirit and body of Christ!

To be set apart, God is telling us to be holy because he is holy (Lev 11:44; 1 Pet 1:13–16). This means the state of purity or integrity of moral character, freedom from sin, and sanctity. When applied to humans, holiness is the purity of heart or dispositions, sanctified affections, righteousness, and moral goodness, *but not perfect*. While we're not perfect, God knows when we're striving toward his righteous ways of living. We cannot be a helpful tool for our Lord when we don't follow the holiness and righteousness of his teachings—100%.

When we commit ourselves to Christ the enemy will attempt to pull us back to our old ways. After all, Satan hates anything that is part of God's holiness. When we look at 1 Pet 1:13–16, it tells us to be set apart from the world because we must be more like our Heavenly Father—holy in everything we do. So, prepare your minds for action and exercise self-control. Put all your hope in the gracious salvation that will come to you when Jesus Christ is revealed to the world. So, you must live as God's obedient children. Don't slip back into your old ways of living to satisfy your desires. You didn't know any better then. But now, you must be holy in everything you do, just as God who chose you is holy. The Scriptures say, "You must be holy because I am holy."

When we lean on the power of the Holy Spirit to empower us and separate us from the ways of the world, he will help us from slipping back into our old ways of living. To be set apart means God chose us specifically for his Glory. Once we realize the magnitude of that purpose and plan, our objectives and perspectives will shift and be more in line with his will.

> Dear friends, do not believe everyone who claims to speak by the Spirit. You must test them to see if the spirit they have comes from God. For there are many false prophets in the world. (1 John 4:1)

---

1. "Are Many Practices and Traditions," paras. 2–3.

WEEK 8

The Big Picture

Gen 36–40

We will never quite understand everything God is doing in our finite minds. But as we continue this journey in week 8, we now see a bigger picture of who we are in Christ and our Heavenly Father's expectations. Throughout this time with the Lord, he wants us to understand what he's doing in our lives so we can clearly see his required plans. This will enable us to better prepare for today and tomorrow, affecting our lives and others around us. But most importantly, our Lord!

Too often, it's difficult to see what God is doing at that very moment in our life. But, if we look back over time, we should realize God has been saving us from situations in which the enemy was planning for our defeat. As we grow in our daily walk with the Lord and see him for Who he is—the bigger picture becomes more precise than ever before. Then we thank him for everything he's doing for us today, and especially in the future.

God knows and sees the beginning and end of the story. He has a plan for you and me that will always be best. We may not see it now, but his big picture will come to life. The key is staying close to the Lord, in the grand scheme of things, and follow every part of his his word. You may jump when you see something getting ready to happen but he tells you to relax, don't get anxious, and trust in Me. That little thing you jumped at holds no candlestick to the Big Plan ahead. *"For as the heavens are high above the earth, so great are His mercy and loving-kindness toward those who reverently and worshipfully fear Him" (Ps 103:11)*

CHAPTER 36

Godly Evidence

> Esau took his wives, his children, and his entire household, along with his livestock and cattle—all the wealth he had acquired in the land of Canaan—and moved away from his brother, Jacob. There was not enough land to support them both because of all the livestock and possessions they had acquired. So, Esau (also known as Edom) settled in the hill country of Seir. (Gen 36:6–8)

Esau was not God's chosen one for the plan of redemption, but he still blessed him. Even when Esau cried to Isaac, "Have you only one blessing, my father?" (Gen 27:38). This proved invalid, for God blessed Esau because he was a descendant of Abraham. But he blessed him in a way that he only cared about, which was more material—not spiritual. Huge point!

The Edomites were Esau's descendants and related to the Israelites, for Esau was the twin brother of Jacob. So, the evidence of family ties was there. However, Edom's actions against God's chosen people, and relatives were repulsive. However, God was still merciful when he told Israel to leave Edom alone, for they were relatives (Deut 2:4–5). Still, Edom refused to let Israel enter their land, and over time, they became bitter enemies of King David.

As time passed, Edom's perpetual conflict with Israel and not following all of God's ways would lead to their destruction. Obadiah prophesied that they would be utterly despised, and the house of Esau would be stubble, and it happened! The Edomites would later disappear from history, for God said whoever curses you, I will curse (Gen 12:3). It was evident that Esau's lineage would not be a part of God's family because of their lack of godliness.

First John 3:9–10 states this so eloquently: "Those who have been born into God's family do not make a practice of sinning, because God's life is in them. So, they can't keep on sinning because they are children of God. How can we tell the difference between the children of God and the children of the devil? Anyone who refuses to live righteously and love other believers does not belong to God."

The evidence of a devoted follower of Christ, is displayed in both faith and action because they are a new person. The old life is gone; a new life has begun!" (2 Cor. 5:17). James says, "I will show you my faith by my good deeds" (Jas 2:18). Jesus said this: "I am the light of the world. If you follow me, you won't have to walk in darkness, because you will have the light that leads to life" (John 8:12).

Genuine Christians will show their faith by how they live in word and deed. They enforce peace and unity within the body, turn from sin to Christ, exemplify humility, and illuminate unconditional love. Grace and mercy are evident in their spiritual lives, and they don't aim to bring discord and disagreement amongst the family of God! They strive to have a pure heart, overcome temptations, and work hard to portray Christlikeness. God's faithful ones know they're not perfect, but work diligently to make sure they minimize their mistakes. Their desire is to make good choices, study and apply the word, and embody the evidence of walking in the ways of their Savior.

It's hard to find fault in a Godly person *when the Lord is first place in their life*. They give a helping hand to those in need and have a prayer life second to none. They possess the unmistakable evidence of Col 3:4: "And when Christ, who is your life, is revealed to the whole world, you will share in all His glory." They intentionally live out their life for the Lord every day.

> Those who say they live in God should live their lives as Jesus did. (1 John 2:6)

CHAPTER 37

Our Role

> Jacob loved Joseph more than any of his other children because Joseph had been born to him in his old age. So, one day Jacob had a special gift made for Joseph—a beautiful robe. But his brothers hated Joseph because their father loved him more than the rest of them. They couldn't say a kind word to him. (Gen 37:3-4)

Jacob loved his son Joseph more than the others because He set him apart with a special gift. Little did his father know he was setting his favorite son up for a storyline that would be discussed for generations because it was part of God's plan. Intertwined in this unbelievable story of mercy, grace, and love is how the main character (Joseph) would point us to our Savior today.

We see a beautiful correlation in the story of one man used by God not because Joseph was the favorite Bible hero that he wanted to emulate, but because God is sovereign. He has been laying the tracks for the glory of Christ throughout redemptive history one person at a time.

The Lord calls and offers you a leading role: "Would you be interested in playing the lead part of a significant storyline?" The Lord says, "This story will be one for the ages; it will have an underlying theme that will point the world to Me." He says, "If you accept this role, you will receive a beautiful robe that shows My favor upon you as the lead actor. It will also showcase you as the appointed one that others can recognize. I will differentiate you from others; the world will know there's something special about you. As the lead character, you will possess sterling attributes parallel to Me—Christ, your Savior. In the eyes of many, they will hail you as a hero." Do you accept this role?

Without hesitation, your response is an adamant yes! How could I ever turn down a role like this? It's one of a lifetime. Then you ask the Lord, "Please share the script with me so I can prepare?" The Lord replies, "There's no script; all you need to do is trust Me and My plan!"

However, the Lord says, "I must forewarn you. You will be stripped of your robe, and your family will mock and hate you. Then, you will be thrown into a well and sold for pieces of silver. Next, you will be enslaved—held in bondage and falsely accused. Finally, you will be thrown into prison, and you will stand before rulers unjustly."

The Lord continues, "But I promise you this! There will be a silver lining at the end of this story! Through all the dark days, fiery trials, tribulations, tests, temptations, pain, and suffering, there will be forgiveness, redemption, restoration, reconciliation, and unfathomable new beginnings. And know this—I will always be with you! You may not feel blessed at the moment, but I will bless you in my timing. But the initial sacrifice is up to you. Do you still accept this pivotal role?"

Would you accept a role like this that had a storyline pointing to the Savior today? Assuming the role as a follower of Jesus Christ is striving to be like him, daily and making him Lord of your life (Rom 10:9; 1 Cor 12:3). Because of God's grace, we want to please him in every Christlike act we perform and we accomplish this when we allow the Holy Spirit to control our lives completely (Eph 5:18).

The crucial role of following Christ means we apply the truths from his word and *live it as if Jesus walked beside us in person every day. He's our Director and Producer in every act we perform!*

> My old self has been crucified with Christ. It is no longer I who live, but Christ lives in me. So I live in this earthly body by trusting in the Son of God, who loved me and gave himself for me. (Gal 2:20)

CHAPTER 38

He's Fair & Faithful

> Judah noticed her and thought she was a prostitute, since she had covered her face. So, he stopped and propositioned her. "Let me have sex with you," he said, not realizing that she was his own daughter-in-law. "How much will you pay to have sex with me?" Tamar asked. "I'll send you a young goat from my flock," Judah promised. "But what will you give me to guarantee that you will send the goat?" she asked. "What kind of guarantee do you want?" he replied. She answered, "Leave me your identification seal and its cord and the walking stick you are carrying." So, Judah gave them to her. Then he had intercourse with her, and she became pregnant. (Gen 38:15–18)

We know this story oh so well. Three months passed, and Judah got word that his daughter-in-law was acting like a prostitute, and Judah exclaimed, "Bring her out and let her be burned!" But as they were taking her out to be killed, Tamar sent a message to Judah, "The man who owns these things made me pregnant," and behold, it was Judah caught red-handed.

Judah even stated Tamar was more righteous than he, for he did not keep his word in allowing his son Shelah to marry Tamar. But also, another key takeaway for us in this story of Judah is *hypocrisy*. Judah was about to kill Tamar for a sin he was equally guilty of. Bottom line—Judah's immoral character, hypocrisy, and lack of integrity resulted in family strife and deception.

Is there any moral value in this story? Where is the spiritual application? Why are some of these stories in the Bible, which are not so pleasant, included in God's word? How could some of these "faithful believers" with all their guilty acts be granted the privilege of being included in the Messianic line, such as the case with Judah and Tamar (Matt 1:1–6)? Even though they were both examples of ungodliness, their son Perez is listed as part of the Messianic line! God's wonderful grace transformed their works into something amazing in their lineage. I think this clearly show us that *God's purpose is accomplished despite man's unrighteousness.*

Sometimes people pose the question, "Is God fair?" The short answer is, "Yes, he is fair." Our God is fair and just in all that He does. No one can ever be equal to His fairness. He is gracious, loving, merciful, and fair in everything. No one, not even the most intelligent person on earth, can grasp what God desires and plans are.

So, to sum it up here's the gut punch for you and me. God loved us so much, regardless of our immoral behaviors, lack of godliness, and hypocrisy, he brought his only Son to save us from a life of torment. Therefore, we must remember that his ways and thoughts are above ours (Isa 55:8-9). In all his Sovereignty—we must trust and believe in his word because he's God—he's Fair, Just, and Faithful!

In Heb 11, there is a long list of Old Testament people who are commended for their faith, and among them are many sinful people who did dreadful things. But, because they believed in God, their faith was credited to them as righteousness (Gen 15:6). There's no *measure to God's grace and mercy for those who live by faith*! So, the big question is this; is your name among those on this list *in the book of life?* He's fair and faithful enough to allow anyone to be included in this book of eternal life when they give their life to his One and only Son—Jesus Christ! No matter who you are or what you've done, his invitation of salvation is always open to the repentant heart.

> Faith shows the reality of what we hope for; it is the evidence of things we cannot see. Through their faith, the people in days of old earned a good reputation. (Heb 11:1-2)

CHAPTER 39

Don't Compromise

> From the day Joseph was put in charge of his master's household and property, the Lord began to bless Potiphar's household for Joseph's sake. All his household affairs ran smoothly, and his crops and livestock flourished. So, Potiphar gave Joseph complete administrative responsibility over everything he owned. With Joseph there, he didn't worry about a thing—except what kind of food to eat! Joseph was a very handsome and well-built young man, and Potiphar's wife soon began to look at him lustfully. "Come and sleep with me," she demanded. But Joseph refused. "Look," he told her, "My master trusts me with everything in his entire household. No one here has more authority than I do. He has held back nothing from me except you because you are his wife. How could I do such a wicked thing? It would be a great sin against God." (Gen 39:5–8)

God was indeed with Joseph and blessed him greatly as he served in the home of his Egyptian master Potiphar, and God even blessed Potiphar for Joseph's sake. All affairs ran smoothly and flourished. With everything going so great, the God-fearing man, Joseph, had complete administrative responsibility for everything the master owned.

But then it happened—out of the blue. His master's wife desired Joseph and lured him to sleep with her. She would continue to pressure him more and more with the temptation. How would you respond to this? This must have been tempting for Joseph because at the heart of the issue is this: Potiphar's wife promised happiness and sensual satisfaction—temptations that an ordinary man cannot flee from when he's in the flesh. But Joseph saw sin for what it is and he refused to act out "this great wickedness." Joseph feared God, knowing that all sin was ultimately against him (see Ps 51:4).

Saying "no" to Potiphar's wife, Joseph showed himself to be a man of Godly wisdom: "The fear of the LORD is the beginning of wisdom; all who follow his precepts have good understanding" (Ps 111:10).

So here we are, charting our life's course, and things are going well; we recognize God's grace and favor and simply love life. Things could not be any better. But, over time—we fall into the danger zone of complacency and comfort, and then it creeps in again. We cry out, "I need to find a way back to the closeness of You, oh God, because now I am bombarded with vulnerable attacks. I've compromised to the ways of the world, and I let my guard down. I am drifting away and feel it in the depths of my soul. Help me, Lord, please reel me in because I am so far apart from your will. . . . I need you now!"

As we go through this life journey, we will hear those calls to compromise the ways of the world. Those "fleeting pleasures of sin" (Heb 11:25), the lust of the flesh, lust of the eyes, and the pride of life (1 John 2:16). They all tempt us to compromise in areas we know we shouldn't.

Usually, the temptation to compromise is heightened by some type of peer pressure. It's when we feel ostracized from the world and apart from our little cliques—we want to get back into the inner circle, and that's when we give in! But no matter what—don't cave into anything, that's not of God!

The enemy's work is to lure us into conforming to the ways of the world, which is opposite of God's plan. We must rely on his enduring strength to help us overcome these times. "For I can do everything through Christ, who gives me strength" (Phil 4:13). The troubles in this life, the pressures, temptations, the trials, and the test of times are coming. But as they come—we must come to Christ and ask him for strength.

Remember these two powerful passages: "Don't love money; be satisfied with what you have. For God has said, 'I will never fail you. I will never abandon you'" (Heb. 13:5) and "The temptations in your life are no different from what others experience. And God is faithful. He will not allow the temptation to be more than you can stand. When you are tempted, he will show you a way out so that you can endure" (1 Cor. 10:13). *We will be less likely to cave into the compromising ways of the world when we realize that God's sufficiency is all we need!*

> Guard your heart above all else, for it determines the course of your life. (Prov 4:23)

CHAPTER 40

God's Timing

> While they were in prison, Pharaoh's cup-bearer and baker each had a dream one night, and each dream had its own meaning. When Joseph saw them the next morning, he noticed that they both looked upset. "Why do you look so worried today?" he asked them. And they replied, "We both had dreams last night, but no one can tell us what they mean." "Interpreting dreams is God's business," Joseph replied. "Go ahead and tell me your dreams." (Gen 40:5–8)

I love the story of Joseph, where he's imprisoned after being unjustly accused. Despite his situation, Joseph felt God was still with him and would continue to bless him. I can only say wow to anyone with so much faith and endurance. Because even in this dark place, Joseph still had the *intestinal fortitude* from God to influence and help people, such as Pharaoh's chief cupbearer and the chief baker. No matter the doom and gloom in his life, Joseph seized the opportunity to be a Godly example for his Lord!

When the cupbearer and chief baker offended their master—they were cast in prison "with Joseph." Joseph saw the sad look on their faces and asked them," why do you look so worried today?" Joseph assisted them both with interpreting their dreams (with God's help), but only the chief cupbearer would receive positive news.

Joseph knew that the good news for the chief cupbearer would restore his position in the master's home, so Joseph asked him to pity him when he was back in favor with the master. But the chief cupbearer forgot, and Joseph would be imprisoned for two more years. But Joseph stayed faithful to his Lord no matter what!

Joseph could have easily not assisted the cupbearer, but Joseph was a God-fearing man; he knew God was with him and would still bless him. Joseph had been blessed by God so many times when death was crouching at his door; he knew by staying connected with God, his Lord would not let him down.

I cannot fathom the despair Joseph may have felt waiting for another two-plus years in that prison. But what God would do in Joseph's life in the coming years would bring renewal and restoration that only our God can. How God placed the cupbearer in Joseph's life—of all places in a prison—would work out God's plan in his perfect timing.

When God places the "right people" in the "right" place and at the "right time," in our lives—there's a formula God has put in place to increase our faith and strengthen our Christian walk when we need it the most. I love it when I see God working through others and then watch his plan come to fruition. It blows me away! He's planted people in our life because it will draw us nearer to him. And we get to witness his wondrous work on display through their acts.

Our "great command" is to love God and our neighbors, and this type of love he orders in our life will open doors for the "right people" we need at just the right time. It is amazing how God can use other Christians—good and bad experiences to help shape us into being more like His Son, especially when we don't let pride get in the way.

Our "God is in the business" of creating life, changing lives, providing spiritual gifts, saving souls, and making all things new. And this reminds me that our God is Sovereign, Faithful, and True. God wants us to reflect his character in a world full of darkness, confusion, and despair, no matter our circumstances in life.

Therefore, our daily acts of "his" business should include a hunger to know him more, love him more, serve him more, and trust him more. Then his character forms within us to the likeness of his Son, Jesus Christ. When we get involved with God's daily business, we can see great things happen at just the right time!

> "For I know the plans I have for you," says the Lord. "They are plans for good and not for disaster, to give you a future and a hope." (Jer 29:11)

WEEK 9

Building Godly Character

Gen 41–45

In this next-to-last week of the journey, evidence of our Christlike character should be noticeable in our daily thoughts, intentions, motives, and desires. There should be a vast improvement in our choice of words and actions—that is more in line with the word of God.

Our old character may have been more influenced by the flesh, but as Christ-followers grow, they yield to his Spirit and put their spiritual gifts into action. They endure and instill God's obedience and develop a godly life that produces fruitful living.

A godly character has a discerning spirit—dissecting right and wrong. Their insight and wisdom lead them to surrender and submit their own will to the Lord and to do what is right in God's sight. Regardless of the pressures and temptations that may come, the traits of a godly character strive to keep their hearts pure and minds sharp (clear of impurities). They possess actions of integrity and humility—using words with wisdom, grace, and love. They're forgiving, do everything without complaining and arguing (peacemakers), and are patient through the storms—devoting themselves to the Lord as Godly stewards.

We develop godly characters when we control our thoughts (Phil 4:8; Col 3:2), practice Christlike behaviors (Gal 5:22–23), guard our hearts (Phil 4:6–7), and surround ourselves with sound believers (2 Cor 6:14)—connected to the "right" community. They exemplify the model of Christlikeness others will want to follow, and it will be evident to everyone around them (Titus 2:7–8).

CHAPTER 41

His Appointed Gifts

The next morning Pharaoh was very disturbed by the dreams. So, he called for all the magicians and wise men of Egypt. When Pharaoh told them his dreams, not one of them could tell him what they meant. Finally, the king's chief cupbearer spoke up. "Today I have been reminded of my failure," he told Pharaoh. "Some time ago, you were angry with the chief baker and me, and you imprisoned us in the palace of the captain of the guard. One night the chief baker and I each had a dream, and each dream had its own meaning. There was a young Hebrew man with us in the prison who was a slave of the captain of the guard. We told him our dreams, and he told us what each of our dreams meant. And everything happened just as he had predicted. I was restored to my position as cupbearer, and the chief baker was executed and impaled on a pole." (Gen 41:8–13)

Nothing evil can do the work of God. While these men may have had power, it was not godly power, for they could not interpret Pharoah's dream. At just the right time, when the chief cupbearer saw his master needed help, he remembered how Joseph—the right person at the right time in the right place (of all places in a prison) could help his master.

Joseph had a unique gift from God, interpreting dreams because he trusted God and knew he was always with him. Still, the dreams he interpreted for the cupbearer, baker, and most specifically, Pharaoh elevated his life on a platform that brought glory to his Lord. Even Pharaoh recognized that Joseph was filled with the spirit of God! Wow!

But here's the critical point! While Joseph was provided with this gift, he always gave attention to God. Even though it benefited him in his high-ranking position in Egypt and freed him from a dungeon, God was always on the pedestal. Joseph used his appointed gifts as a platform and turned it into a powerful witness for the Lord.

When Pharaoh heard about Joseph's gift, he demanded to see him immediately. Joseph was brought from the dungeon with no preparation and not knowing the purpose of the master's request. Yet, Joseph was ready for almost anything because of his right relationship with God. It was not Joseph's knowledge of the dreams that helped him to interpret them; it was his knowledge of God. And that closeness and trust he had in knowing God's business prepared him for a life-changing moment.

How does the world recognize Christlike attributes in us? Are our gifts so profound and pronounced that they're recognized by those who are unbelievers or even our enemies? The dark world can see the light of Christ in us through his unconditional love, choice of words and Christlike actions. Doing God's daily business may seem daunting and challenging at times, but we can do it by his grace.

God grants us lives filled with many blessings and opportunities—and the people he's placed around us could be God's timing and plan to come to fruition. God's purpose is for us to live an active and intentional life for his glory, utilizing our unique gifts daily. But the key is this—how close are we walking with our Lord daily!

Because those gifts will seem distant and useless if we're far from our Lord—not allowing his Spirit to work in us. If we are not consistently focusing on God, we can easily fall away by thinking about the things of this world. Way too often the gifts of the world are more of a focus than his gifts at work in us. We must continually seek God and his righteousness as our only source of all that we need and want (1 Chr 16:11). When he's our ultimate focus his gifts are fresh—alive and ready to be used.

> God has given each of you a gift from his great variety of spiritual gifts. Use them well to serve one another. (1 Pet 4:10)

CHAPTER 42

Spirit Trumps Flesh

> Since Joseph was governor of all Egypt and in charge of selling grain to all the people, it was to him that his brothers came. When they arrived, they bowed before him with their faces to the ground. Joseph recognized his brothers instantly, but he pretended to be a stranger and spoke harshly to them. "Where are you from?" he demanded. "From the land of Canaan," they replied. "We have come to buy food." Although Joseph recognized his brothers, they didn't recognize him. (Gen 42:6–8)

Joseph could have revealed his identity to his brothers. After all, his last memory of his brothers was staring in horror at them as the slave traders carried him away. However, Joseph decided to be rough with them and put them through tests to determine if they were the same evil and jealous brothers he once knew. Through this ordeal with his brothers, no matter what, he is still faithful to the Lord, as stated in Gen 41:38.

The glorious truth of God's providence is that he can and will use man's evil actions to further his good purpose and plan. However, this never excuses man's evil. *It means God's wisdom and goodness are greater than man's evil* because "The eyes of the Lord are in every place, watching the evil and the good" (Prov 15:3).

Joseph could have easily succumbed to the flesh, acted out in rage, anger, and unforgiveness, and even plotted their deaths as his brothers did earlier in his life. Still, Joseph's close relationship with God would supersede any fleshly moves, for this was all part of God's plan.

Reading about where Joseph's brothers masked their sins to Jacob led me to the battle of flesh and Spirit. It brought me to this question: "Are we wearing a mask that prevents the world from seeing who we are in Christ?"

So, here we are in a world crazing over a new wave of thinking and doing things. And today, more than ever, the Lord needs his lightness in and through us revealed for the unbelieving and dark world to see.

God's word tells us in Gal 5 there are only two forces constantly in conflict and they "cannot coexist"—they are the flesh and the Spirit. So, who's controlling us? Who's the real victor in our daily lives?

So, to keep this straightforward, the critical focus is on two areas: barriers and connection. 1) Are we allowing barriers to prevent us from living God's intended life? 2) Or is our connection with the Lord enabling us to overcome those barriers?

Here's the sting—when these barriers control us, they will throw up the masking walls in our lives. And the enemy will use these vices to display our inability to understand what God wants: and that is to trust and obey him wholeheartedly and follow all his ways!

When we peel back all the ugly barriers, too many hideous vices surface, such as pride, jealousy/envy, anger, worry, hatred, division, murder, gossip, lying, stealing, manipulating, deceiving, drunkenness, guilt, fear, anxiety, impatience, doubt, depression, aggression, failure, insecurity, sexual immorality, stinking thinking and nothing but self-ambitions. The enemy has a dirty laundry list on us!

It's sad to see the world championing so much pride in today's world and just as sad—man falls prey to it. We're seeing a society of individuals wanting to exalt themselves and push our Lord right out of the big scheme of things. The reason is simply this—they have a barrier called "their agenda." There's nothing Christlike in their intent. But the Lord has called you and me to be the opposite of what this country and world are doing. He wants a daily connection with us so they can see his powerful and amazing grace seen through our humbleness.

At the core of what James tells us in chapter 4 of his epistle is this: "Drawing close to God is humility—the attitude of our hearts." "Humble yourselves before the Lord, and He will lift you up in honor" (Jas 4:10). And we all know the opposite of humility, and that's pride. And James also tells us in this chapter that God opposes the proud but gives grace to the humble, which is our key takeaway.

When we humble ourselves before God, yield to the power of his Spirit, resist the ways of the world and its prideful ways, and ground ourselves in the Truth of his word—He's then exalted because of what we allow him to do in our lives. He's now magnified, not the world, because of his work in and through us. And that's when he will lift us up in honor.

So, I pose this question to the community. "Who would not want to be lifted in honor by the Lord and have victory over the barriers in their life?"

They will fight you, but they will fail. For I am with you, and I will take care of you. I, the Lord, have spoken. (Jer 1:19)

CHAPTER 43

Faith Trumps Fear

> Also take double the money that was put back in your sacks, as it was probably someone's mistake. Then take your brother and go back to the man. May God Almighty give you mercy as you go before the man, so that he will release Simeon and let Benjamin return. But if I must lose my children, so be it. (Gen 43:12–14)

When Jacob's sons returned from their trip to Egypt—only to find the money in their grain sacks that they used to pay for the grain was still there (uh oh), months would pass when they would need to return for more food. So, Jacob instructed them to take extra (based on his experiences). But you can't help but notice his torn heart.

He conceded to his sons and allowed Benjamin to go. He even said, "but if I lose my children, so be it." Believing he had lost his favorite son and now the possibility of his youngest and others, he had it in himself to pray for God to have mercy upon them. But how steadfast was his genuine faith? Was he too concerned about the fatality of losing his sons? Because faith and fatalism (the inevitable) don't go hand in hand.

Genuine faith is a complete trust or confidence in someone or something. We build trust and confidence in the Lord over time as he repeatedly proves himself. You would think after all Jacob had gone through and experienced by the work of God's hand, his faith would have been more steadfast. Could it be he was seeing more of a bleak future with the famine and fatalities—and that's now consumed his heart and mind?

Change and troubles will hit us like the wind, and they can impact us from every direction of life. It's inevitable, not if, but when. James 1:2 reminds us, "Dear brothers and sisters, when troubles of any kind come your way, consider it an opportunity for great joy."

James is telling us that "when" calamity comes, there's a way we can profit from them. And that is not dwelling on the negative but having a more positive outlook and "knowing" that all things will work together for the good—for those who love the Lord and are called according to His purpose and plan (Rom 8:28).

When we lack faith, we need to turn these hardships into learning stages of patience, endurance, and perseverance. The only adaptation we can choose to learn from is through our faith and the foundation of God's word—and yielding to his power.

Suppose we learn from our convictions and counseling through the Holy Spirit. In that case, we will find more of his wisdom and knowledge—and experience his peace. And that kind of peace is our safeguard because it protects our hearts and mind from the horror and evil surrounding us today that can also steal our joy (Phil 4:7).

As our faith continues to grows in our daily walk with the Lord—more of his nature is revlealed to us. A Christ-centered faith results from a life being refined, reshaped, and molded by him. Our lives will change and reflect more of him through the test of time.

> These trials will show that your faith is genuine. It is being tested as fire tests and purifies gold—though your faith is far more precious than mere gold. So when your faith remains strong through many trials, it will bring you much praise and glory and honor on the day when Jesus Christ is revealed to the whole world. (1 Pet 1:7)

CHAPTER 44

Overcome Suffering

When his brothers were ready to leave, Joseph instructed his palace manager: "Fill each of their sacks with as much grain as they can carry and put each man's money back into his sack. Then put my personal silver cup at the top of the youngest brother's sack, along with the money for his grain." So, the manager did as Joseph instructed him. (Gen 44:1-2)

The brothers were in high spirits, feeling their journey was a great success, and now ready to return to their father. Simeon's released from prison, their sacks full of grain, and they were treated well. What more could they ask?

But a twist of fate! Joseph would order his men to place his silver cup in the bag of his true full brother Benjamin preparing to put them through the test. Just when they thought all was going smooth, the walls came tumbling down.

Joseph's silver cup symbolized his authority, and to take it was a severe crime. This cup had apparent supernatural powers for the leader's use. They would pour water in it, and the ripples, reflections, and bubbles had a meaning for the future. Still, Joseph didn't need this cup's power because he had the power of God, who helped him to know and foretell future events. But he used this cup to test his brothers! He would see just how much suffering they could endure. So, who would break first, Jacob and his sons—or Joseph?

Of all the challenges thrown at Christians today, suffering may be the most difficult to explain. Throughout God's word, we see many great examples of dealing with grief, loss, and pain. We've seen an excellent portrayal of suffering in the life of Joseph in Genesis. But probably one of the most famous illustrations is in the book of Job! Because it's an unbelievable story of riches to rags to riches!

Job suffers because the enemy tells God the only reason Job is trusting Him is because of his wealth and that everything in life is going well. So, the testing of Job's faith began. First, Satan "was allowed" to destroy all of Job's possessions, except for his wife. But all was lost! Then the enemy was allowed to attack Job himself. *But no matter what, Job trusted God!*

Did Job have moments of weakness? Yes! He allowed his suffering to overwhelm him and question God. And it's not until that point when Job rests on nothing but the faithfulness of God and the hope of his redemption he would come to be patient and endure—and experience God's blessing after the test: "[The Lord] gave him twice as much as he had before" (Job 42:10).

So, in this story, we see that a significant purpose for suffering is to try our faith because God rates our faith very highly; because without faith, it is impossible to please God (Heb 11:6). The Christian life is all about faith; it is "from faith to faith" as noted in (Rom 1:17).

Also, when we're going through times of suffering, God is trying to get our attention because he always has a better outcome for us—as he did with Job. Not saying this from a worldly point of view, but spiritually. We cannot see the road ahead, which will include discomfort, but it will consist of joy, peace, and spiritual growth—because through it all, our Lord wants a growing relationship with us– as he did since the beginning of time.

God's original purpose for humanity was one with a beautiful friendship, relationship, complete joy, and obedience to him. But mankind's pride and one fatal choice led to an estrangement—a choice that distorted us from the true image of God! The consequences left us with a defected, diseased, and dying body—leading us to suffer brokenness, constant frustration, loss, and bitter division amongst all levels of society. We're always in a state of confusion, aimlessness, and continued strife and sometimes overwhelmed with emotional and spiritual defeat.

First, we must realize on this side of heaven, we will struggle with heartache, pain, loss, and suffering. We will experience injustice, inhumane ways, defiance, and rebellious acts. We will observe trouble, dissension, discord, and division, and it will seem to become an ordinary way of life. None of this was part of God's original plan for humanity! Because man fell from his original position in the garden of Eden. We now live in a fallen and corrupt world, and all creation "moans and groans" under the consequences of our sin and wrongdoings (Rom 8:22).

Like all other human experiences, suffering is directed by God's sovereign wisdom. Ultimately, we may never know the specific reason for our suffering. However, still, we must trust in our sovereign God, *which is the real answer to suffering* (Rom 8:28).

In our moments of the flesh—we will feel that suffering has led us to the end of our rope. With no hope in sight! But the good news is that God does not intend us to groan forever. Through Jesus Christ, God is repairing us for a new creation—a place with no more pain and suffering. He will set all things right for those who belong to his Son. What a wonderful promise of eternal hope! Because in his divine providence, God orchestrates every event in our lives—even suffering, temptation, and sin—to accomplish both our temporal and eternal benefit. In the long run, you may not sense or feel it, but *it's worth it in the end!* As we go through times of suffering, we must remember this powerful passage: "Yet what we suffer now is nothing compared to the glory he will reveal to us later" (Rom 8:18).

> In his kindness God called you to share in his eternal glory by means of Christ Jesus. So after you have suffered a little while, he will restore, support, and strengthen you, and he will place you on a firm foundation. (1 Pet 5:10)

CHAPTER 45

Real Love

Joseph could stand it no longer. There were many people in the room, and he said to his attendants, "Out, all of you!" So, he was alone with his brothers when he told them who he was. Then he broke down and wept. He wept so loudly the Egyptians could hear him, and word of it quickly carried to Pharaoh's palace. "I am Joseph!" he said to his brothers. "Is my father still alive?" But his brothers were speechless! They were stunned to realize that Joseph was standing there in front of them. "Please, come closer," he said to them. So, they came closer. And he said again, "I am Joseph, your brother, whom you sold into slavery in Egypt. But don't be upset, and don't be angry with yourselves for selling me to this place. It was God who sent me here ahead of you to preserve your lives." (Gen 45:1–5)

The power of forgiveness, reconciliation, restoration, redemption, and genuine love is conveyed and portrayed "for our good" in these passages. Love keeps no record, and it's apparent in Joseph's tale between him and his brothers! He never had to reveal his identity or that he was one of the most powerful men in Egypt at the time—because he had it all going for him. But the power of God at work in him—working out his plan—should be our user guide today in forgiveness and reconciliation. It is one for the ages—laid out beautifully in God's word!

His great emotion showed that Joseph did not manipulate his brothers. God directed him to make these arrangements, and it hurt him to do so. Joseph told them he was their brother and perhaps showed them some scars or birthmarks characteristic of their real brother. Sound familiar? Jesus showed his scars to a doubting Thomas, for he did not believe. Once you truly believe your faith and love are wholeheartedly committed, that is faith working through love (Gal 5:6).

God's realm best defines genuine love as "agape love." The essence of agape love is goodwill, benevolence, and willful delight in the object of love. The type of love that characterizes God is not a sappy or sentimental feeling because his love portrays his nature and the expression of his supernatural being. *He loves the unlovable and the unlovely.* Not because we deserve to be loved or of any excellence we possess, it is God's nature to love and he must be faithful to his true character.

Agape love does not come naturally because of our fallen sinful nature. Therefore, we are incapable of producing such a Godly love. If we are to love as God loves, that agape love can only come from its Source—a love that "has been poured out into our hearts through the Holy Spirit, who has been given to us" when we became his children (Rom 5:5; Gal 5:22). "This is how we know what love is: Jesus Christ laid down his life for us. And we ought to lay down our lives for our brothers and sisters" (1 John 3:16). Because of God's love toward us, we can love one another.

The greatest of all things that will endure the test of times is love! First Corinthians 13:4-7 says, "Love is patient and kind. Love is not jealous or boastful or proud, or rude. It does not demand its way. It is not irritable, and it keeps no record of being wronged. It does not rejoice about injustice but rejoices whenever the truth wins out. Love never gives up, loses faith, is always hopeful, and endures through every circumstance."

Christlike *love* is charitable, generous, unconditional, and selfless. Here are some challenging questions. What is the true love of your life? How do you recognize it? How would you measure this one true love? Because the real measuring stick is that it will drive our devotion inwardly and outwardly—one that expresses an enthusiasm of intense and eager enjoyment—every minute of every day!

Now—how does that love of something or someone compare to your love for Jesus Christ? Always remember that love is essential to God and listed as the first Fruit of the Spirit. The greatest commandment is in Matt 22:37-39, *"Love the Lord your God with all your heart, soul, and mind. This is the first and greatest commandment. A second is equally important: Love your neighbors as yourself."* So, is Christlike love, his agape love, reigning in your daily life?

- Longing—an intense and undeniable yearning and burning desire!
- Obedient—willing to comply; submissive and conforming to his authority!

- Valid—sound and factual; clear evidence and proof!
- Everlasting—endless!

> So now I am giving you a new commandment: Love each other. Just as I have loved you, you should love each other. (John 13:34)

WEEK 10

Blessed Relations

Gen 46–50

In this last week of our journey, our daily steps with the Lord should have strengthened our relationship. It should yield a clear understanding of his Sovereignty in our lives (his supreme power and authority). Walking daily with God brings peace and comfort. We see fewer complications knowing that through the storms and test of time, our Father is Perfect and understands what's best for us. We can lean on his divine instructions to help us overcome temptations because he only wants his goodness in our lives.

Having a personal relationship with God begins when we realize our need for him, admit we are sinners, and receive Jesus Christ as our Savior in faith. God, our heavenly Father, has always desired to be close and have a relationship with us. Those who have a personal relationship with God include him in their daily lives. They pray to him, read his word, and meditate on verses to get to know him better. Trusting in God to get us through each day and believing that he is our Sustainer is the way to have a relationship with him through his Son.

Through the power of his Spirit and the application of his word, we have daily aliveness because they enlighten us, and we delight in them with joy, hope, and encouragement. Then we return to him—prayers, acts of gratitude, resolutions to battle the fight of faith—and show our acts of obedience through genuine love. This will reflect the closeness of Christ in us, and establish the blessed relationship we long to experience every day.

CHAPTER 46

Know His Sovereignty

> So, Jacob set out for Egypt with all his possessions. And when he came to Beersheba, he offered sacrifices to the God of his father, Isaac. During the night God spoke to him in a vision. "Jacob! Jacob!" he called. "Here I am," Jacob replied. "I am God, the God of your father," the voice said. "Do not be afraid to go down to Egypt, for there I will make your family into a great nation. I will go with you down to Egypt, and I will bring you back again. You will die in Egypt, but Joseph will be with you to close your eyes." (Gen 46:1–4)

Jacob has received the news that his favorite son, Joseph, is still alive. Through the power of God's grace and mercy, he has brought the story full circle and will bring them together again. God tells Jacob to travel to a distant and *unknown land*, but do you think that uncertainty would overcome the exuberant joy Jacob is feeling? Even if Jacob had any reservations, God reassured him he would go and be with him, and make his family a great nation. What a promise! Jacob knew Egypt was a mighty nation, and they did not believe in the same God he believed in, but he went by faith by hearing the word of God speak to him.

Jacob also knew that God told Abraham his descendants would be strangers in a land that was not theirs. And they would serve them and afflict them for four hundred years (Gen 15:13). Jacob led his family into this foreign land, but he did not know the future. Yet, he knew the future was in God's hands, and he was in complete control. That is a big wow!

How would you react if you knew that your family was embarking upon a new journey that would lead to years of entrapment? In absolute fear—or trusting in God's sovereign ways? Before we can learn to trust that God is in control of our life's circumstances, we must answer five key questions:

1. Do we know and believe that God is in control of our daily life?
2. How much power does he have in my life? How do I know?
3. If God is not in control of my life, who or what is?
4. How can I learn to trust that he is in control—and rest in his grace?
5. Do I lean upon the promises of his word to help me feel reassured?

Some people find it appealing to think Satan controls a certain amount of life and that God is constantly revising His plans to accommodate Satan's tricks. The book of Job is a clear illustration of just who has sovereign power and who doesn't. Satan came to God and, in effect, said, "Job only serves you because you protect him." So God gave Satan permission to do certain things to Job but no more (Job 1:6–22). Could Satan do more than that? No. God is in control over Satan and his demons who try to thwart God's plans at every step.[1]

Our Almighty God is *all-powerful, all-present, and all-knowing*. His power has no restrictions, his majestic throne is unmatched, and no one can thwart his plans! Our God is in complete control of all circumstances, causing or allowing them to fulfill his good purpose and plan—as he wills. His true sovereignty and undeniable ability to enact his will, wherever and however he chooses to come to fruition, clearly shows us Who is genuinely the Ruler of life!

Finally, the only way to trust in God's sovereign control and rest in it—is to know God intimately, personally, and lovingly through his word. We come to know his attributes through his word and that builds confidence in our relationship with him. Daniel 11:32 (NASB) says, "The people who know their God shall be strong and take action."

Paul even reminds us of this in Col 3:16–17. Suppose we let the words of Christ in all their richness, live in our hearts and make us wise. In that case, it will lead us to sing psalms of praise and will lead us to be true representatives of our Lord Jesus, all the while giving thanks through him to God the Father. In every aspect and activity of our daily life, it will be clear Who is Lord of our life!

"Can two people walk together, without agreeing on the direction?" (Amos 3:3). This powerful and short passage is at the heart of knowing that you an intimate, personal, and loving connection with Almighty God—and believing in his direction for your every step in life.

1. "How Can I Learn to Trust," para. 5.

The power punch lies in this commitment. Is that we wish to keep the company of our Lord side-by-side, trusting and knowing he's going to lead us down the right road, to the right place, for the right purpose. And his supremacy, ultimate power, and goodwill are at work and will be completed for our benefit. There's nothing better than knowing that we have a Sovereign God Who is faithful through it all—to the end.

> You can make many plans, but the Lord's purpose will prevail.
> (Prov 19:21)

CHAPTER 47

Coming Together

> Then Joseph went to see Pharaoh and told him, "My father and my brothers have arrived from the land of Canaan. They have come with all their flocks and herds and possessions, and they are now in the region of Goshen." Joseph took five of his brothers with him and presented them to Pharaoh. And Pharaoh asked the brothers, "What is your occupation?" They replied, "We, your servants, are shepherds, just like our ancestors. We have come to live here in Egypt for a while, for there is no pasture for our flocks in Canaan. The famine is very severe there. So please, we request permission to live in the region of Goshen." Then Pharaoh said to Joseph, "Now that your father and brothers have joined you here, choose any place in the entire land of Egypt for them to live. Give them the best land of Egypt. Let them live in the region of Goshen. And if any of them have special skills, put them in charge of my livestock, too." (Gen 47:5-6)

As we approach the end of this journey in Genesis—what a beautiful chapter that shows the power of one man's unbelievable faith, for it would fulfill God's plan and achieve Joseph's desires. The family of Jacob has finally come together in the land of Egypt—they have been reunited as one.

This blessing was all because of Joseph's steadfast faith in God and yielding to his guidance. First, he saved Egypt—and much of the world—from a horrific famine. And now, the whole family of Israel was blessed and would receive an inheritance because of Joseph's relationship with God.

Joseph's incredible and undeniable faithfulness had a massive impact on his entire family and his earthly master, for Pharaoh experienced Joseph's complete devotion and faith in God. Look at the end of this passage where Pharaoh says, if any of his brothers had special skills, *"put them in charge of my livestock, too."* What is so powerful about this is that Egyptians looked down on herdsmen in those days. But because of Joseph, even the greatest leader on earth would yield to the desires of Joseph's family.

Though Joseph experienced many trials throughout his life, he endured and persevered because of his genuine faith in God. His steadfast faith took precedence over all the baggage he could have carried and would bring forth one of the greatest Old Testament stories in the Bible because woven into this story is reconciliation. To see this family of God come together after twenty-plus years of being apart is a reunion that brought forth healing and restoration.

I love Macmillan's definition of "come together": "if people or groups come together, they meet or join in order to do something."[1] God's word reminds us in Heb 10:25 of the importance of coming together—where we share our faith and help strengthen one another in the Lord because of our inheritance in Christ.

So, this question comes to the surface: *What steps can we take in coming together as one where we can be faithful and effective Christians . . . impacting others for God's glory?*

"Come now, let's settle this," says the Lord. "Though your sins are like scarlet, I will make them as white as snow. Though they are red like crimson, I will make them as white as wool. If you will only obey me, you will have plenty to eat. But if you turn away and refuse to listen, you will be devoured by the sword of your enemies. I, the Lord, have spoken!" (Isa 1:18–20)

When we need answers in life, isn't it a blessing to know that God invites us to come before his throne of love, mercy, and grace, anytime and anywhere?

Early in our lives, we may not see God at work through all the trials, tribulations, and tests. Still, in that close relationship we're building—when he sees us through the storms, we will witness his Almighty Hands at work. God will allow things to happen in our lives to bring his purpose and plan to fruition, and when it comes to the surface, it will impact you and others in glorious ways—like Joseph!

When the Holy Spirit is working in our life and sanctifying us, he's setting us apart from our flesh and worldliness to be more like Jesus Christ—so we can stay united in him—working all our effective gifts together in the body, so they are exceptionally pleasing in his eyes! He's bringing us more in line with His holiness because he wants us to dwell in his Presence. And when we abide in our Lord—and him in us, that is when his Son, Jesus Christ, is revealed in our lives.

---

1. C.v. "come together," second definition: https://www.macmillandictionary.com/us/dictionary/american/come-together.

And that's the answer—John 15:4 tells us, "Remain in me, and I will remain in you. For a branch cannot produce fruit if it is severed from the vine, and you cannot be fruitful unless you remain in me." Jesus invites us to come unto him and learn of him. He wants to produce a life that will impart all of him in and through us. He reminds us, "And I am certain that God, who began the good work within you, will continue his work until it is finally finished on the day when Christ Jesus returns" (Phil 1:6). We must submit to the power of his working Spirit to produce all he wants to accomplish in our lives.

When we're in Christ, it affects our decision-making because the Holy Spirit is molding and shaping us. However, we will fall short in our life "for we all fall short of God's glorious standards" (Rom 3:23). And if we make the wrong decision, don't despair, for all is not lost (Isa 41:13; 2 Cor 4:8).

Instead, we can trust God's faithfulness to set us back on the right course. God's sovereign control does not mean we sit idly by and allow life to pass us by. It means that we can go willingly, boldly, and confidently into life (2 Tim 1:7), trusting that our loving Father sees the larger picture and working everything together for his glory.

As we mature in our faith, things in life become more apparent. It will change our perspective and attitude and make a massive impact on our lives and, most importantly, our Lord! When Joseph was thrown in that pit and sold into slavery at seventeen—little did he know how the power of his faith would impact so many lives over twenty years later! And that story of faith would carry on throughout the history of humankind!

Impact is an *I*ndividual-*M*aking-*P*ositive-*A*ttitudes-*C*hristlike-*T*oday!

> Furthermore, because we are united with Christ, we have received an inheritance from God, for he chose us in advance, and he makes everything work out according to his plan. (Eph 1:11)

CHAPTER 48

Perfect Father

> "Now I am claiming as my sons these two boys of yours, Ephraim, and Manasseh, who were born here in the land of Egypt before I arrived. They will be my sons, just as Reuben and Simeon are." Joseph moved the boys, who were at their grandfather's knees, and bowed to the ground with his face. Then he positioned the boys in front of Jacob. With his right hand, he directed Ephraim toward Jacob's left hand, and with his left hand, he put Manasseh at Jacob's right hand. But Jacob crossed his arms as he reached out to lay his hands on the boys' heads. He put his right hand on the head of Ephraim, though he was the younger boy, and his left hand on the head of Manasseh, though he was the firstborn. (Gen 48:5, 12–14)

In this passage, we see where Jacob would give Ephraim the greater blessing instead of his older brother Manasseh. Yet, when Joseph objected—Jacob refused to listen. Why? Because God told Jacob that Ephraim would become greater, so Jacob knew the correct choice, even though it was out of the norm. A key takeaway is when we know God's plan, we're in that close-knit relationship and heeding his voice; we will make favorable choices in life.

The right hand in the Bible always has the idea of the favored position because it is generally considered the hand of strength and skill. Israel (Jacob) knew precisely what he intended to do: to grant a greater blessing to the younger by placing his right hand on Ephraim's head. This practice of blessing the younger over the eldest was against standard customs and expectations during these days. But regardless of what is customary according to the world's standards, God's standards, expectations, and plans are always at the forefront and will always come to fruition.

The name "Manasseh" means forgetfulness, while the name "Ephraim" means fruitfulness (Gen 41:51-52). Some scholars today refer to Ephraim's name as advancement and growth—doubly fruitful. In God's infinite wisdom and his perfect will, he always sees the bigger picture in a person! Never be surprised by what God can do in his perfect plan with anyone.

What are some key takeaways for us in this story? First, in God's word, we can learn from the tribe of Ephraim—(and the other tribes) about our human nature and qualities—who we are as people. The history of the early Israelites is an accurate portrait and reflection of humankind's imperfect and sinful nature that we see today. From the tribes, we see a broad range of similar human behaviors, such as pride, jealousy, and self-centeredness. We even see Ephraim turning away from God and doing wicked things, as recorded in Isa 28:1-3. Yet, we also find the Ephraimites—and even the other tribes, at times recognizing the need to repent and obey God.

When God's plan does not align with ours, do we pout, moan or groan—or do we yearn for his glory and perfect plan to come to fruition? Do we control our pride and jealousy—and accept God's will? Many of us, like the Ephraimites, have difficulty learning those lessons of application. God says we should accept what happens to us as his will, regardless of how good, bad, or ugly those circumstances may seem.

Maybe one of the greatest lessons for us to take away from the history of Ephraim is that God loves us as the Perfect Father—despite all our failings in life. In his perfect plan, choice, timing, and all his patience, and mercy, he has one for you and me that will fit into his sovereign will.

We may not see and understand it at that moment in time, but it is his prescriptive will. So to experience that perfect communion, he may reel us in (Jer 30:22) so we can see and know that he is our Perfect Father and God—all the time! Always remember—in and through it all—he has made us right in his sight—with great things to come!

> For everyone has sinned; we all fall short of God's glorious standard. Yet God, in His grace, freely makes us right in His sight. He did this through Christ Jesus when he freed us from the penalty for our sins. (Rom 3:23-24)

CHAPTER 49

Instructions for His Appointed

> Then Jacob called together all his sons and said, "Gather around me, and I will tell you what will happen to each of you in the days to come. Come and listen, you sons of Jacob, listen to Israel, your father." (Gen 49:1–2)

Jacob is preparing for his death, blessing each of his sons and then making a prediction about each one's future. This would be Jacob's last significant act as a patriarch and the heir to Abraham and Isaac. Here, he prophesied blessings upon each son, one by one. How they lived would play an essential role in Jacob's blessings and prophecy for each son. Psalm 78:5 says, "For he issued His laws to Jacob; He gave his instructions to Israel. He commanded our ancestors to teach them to their children."

If you could see your future family plans today, would you want to know how it plays out? Just like with Jacob's sons, their life choices in how they lived would play a significant role in the prophecy of their lineage. For example, the oldest son, Reuben, was supposed to receive a double inheritance. Still, Reuben lost his special honor, for he chose to sleep with one of his father's concubines. Because of that choice, Jacob could not give the special birthright to a dishonorable son.

The Bible is clear; we cannot only choose but have the responsibility to choose wisely. In the Old Testament, God chose a nation (Israel). However, the people within that nation still had an obligation to choose obedience to God. If they decided to oppose God's plan, it could separate them from the family of God. Still, we must never forget this critical point in our everyday life decisions: Always yield to his guidance for understanding in making choices that align with his will and plan.

So many of us have passed down incomparable qualities that our parents, grandparents, and even great-grandparents taught us. Why? Because at the core of those values, we knew they possessed gems of genuine integrity and authenticity. There was an attraction to those old moral behaviors that were invaluable. We gravitated to them and longed for those precious traits with a desire and passion to pass them on to our children. Why? Because they were ingrained in us, embedded in our minds, and we don't want to let them go. We feel compelled and responsible for passing them down to future generations—hoping that our children would take them to heart, live by them, and pass them down. They are as dear to us now as they were then.

But the first and most important instruction and trait we should encourage and pass down to our children is our action in following Jesus Christ. It will be the best decision we will ever make for the heritage of our lineage. So often, we fall into the trap of wanting to hang on to those old values that "we feel" are the best path for our family. There's nothing wrong with many of those values—if they align with biblical principles and God's teachings.

We must consider what's most important for our families today and in the future and that's our Christ-following character. Second Corinthians 3:7–11 reminds us, "So if the old way, which has been replaced, was glorious, how much more glorious is the new, which remains forever! Since this new way gives us such confidence, we can be very bold." In this passage, Paul reminds the believers that true Christianity is far superior to the Old Testament and any other religion or belief. Why? Because God's plan is far better for us than any other belief. And here's the critical point: we should not reject it or take it casually.

God's word gives us great instructions in Prov chapter 3 and is the perfect guide. In this remarkable book of wisdom, we must seek his will in all we do to receive and understand God's guidance, turning everything in our lives over to him. It's difficult because our flesh wants to control the outcome(s)—way too often. However, the Holy Spirit works in and through a person's will to regenerate that person (John 1:12–13) and give them a new nature. "Put on your new nature, created to be like God—righteous and holy" (Eph 4:24). Salvation is God's work as being part of his family.

We all long for our close ones to make the right decisions in life that will prove they're part of God's family. The key is ensuring Christ is the base for all their decision-making because in him lies the foundation for all pure living and moral choices, for he is our security blanket. He is the pattern to which we should conform to every day—no deviations. Otherwise, man's perceptions of what they see as morally right are at the mercy of their own opinion. And in God's eyes—his Son is our appointed Guide to follow.

Our motives, desires, and actions are voluntary, and we are held responsible for them daily. We must examine our priorities, reasons, passion, and ultimate purpose and objectives and ensure that Jesus Christ is at the center of everything (2 Cor 13:5), aligning with God's commands in our hearts. There will be a disconnect with our Lord if his words are not longing and satisfied within our spirit. We will know it and we will feel it. He tells us to wear them like a necklace, write them deep in our hearts, and never let loyalty and kindness get away. When our loyalty hinges on "our outcome," and that is the only way to satisfy us, the course we're on is not part of God's plan. We must always be in line with his instructed will. "I take joy in doing your will, my God, for your instructions are written on my heart" (Ps 40:8).

> I knew you before I formed you in your mother's womb. Before you were born I set you apart and appointed you as my prophet to the nations. (Jer 1:5)

CHAPTER 50

Good Trumps Evil

After burying Jacob, Joseph returned to Egypt with his brothers and all who had accompanied him to his father's burial. But now that their father was dead, Joseph's brothers became fearful. "Now Joseph will show his anger and pay us back for all the wrong we did to him," they said. So, they sent this message to Joseph: "Before your father died, he instructed us to say to you: 'Please forgive your brothers for the great wrong they did to you—for their sin is oppressing you.' So, we, the servants of the God of your father, beg you to forgive our sin." When Joseph received the message, he broke down and wept. Then his brothers came and threw themselves down before Joseph. "Look, we are your slaves!" they said. But Joseph replied, "Don't be afraid of me. Am I God, that I can punish you? You intended to harm me, but God intended it all for good. He brought me to this position so I could save the lives of many people. No, don't be afraid. I will continue to take care of you and your children." So, he reassured them by speaking kindly to them. (Gen 50:14–21)

The brothers feared Joseph might turn on them after Jacob's death because, let's face it—in our human nature, this was possible. In the passage above, the brothers stated, "He may repay us for all the evil which we did to him." Here, they acknowledged all the evil they did to Joseph. And they worried about the possibility of impending justice—and feared "righteous" retribution. Joseph, with his high status and prestige in Egypt, was capable and had the authority to bring this retribution to his brother's life.

When Joseph wept, it was probably because his brothers thought so little of him and doubted his character. Then, they fell before his face and said, "Behold, we are your servants." They backed up their plea for mercy with a genuine display of humility. Sometimes it takes us to see the ropes of death to bring us to our knees in humility!

Joseph first understood it was not his place but God's to bring retribution upon his brothers—because he knew God was God, and he wasn't. In this passage, "As for you, you meant evil against me; but God meant it for good," Joseph was not glamorizing the wrong his brothers did. He plainly said, "You meant evil against me." Yes, this was true, but here's the most significant truth: "God meant it for good." Romans 8:28 says, "And we know that God causes everything to work together, for the good of those who love God and are called according to his purpose for them."

Many of us could say someone has mistreated us in some shape or form. And with that mistreatment derived family feuds and conflicts that run so deep "no one person" could repair the damage. Sadly, others can allow the enemy to deceive them into doing exactly what he wants—divide and destroy. Unfortunately, in our lifetime, we're going to deal with difficult people; it is unavoidable. When we deal with them it's easy to respond in the flesh, which brings out the worst in us. By the grace of God, may we deal with troublesome people in love, joy, peace, patience, kindness, goodness, faith, gentleness, and—to top it all off—self-control (Gal 5:22–23). May we extend the same love, grace, and mercy that God extended to us. And we must be careful not to become the "difficult people" ourselves!

Sometimes when a difficult person mistreats us, we want to repay them with vengeance. What good comes from paying evil for evil? We all know in the depths of our spirit that it is not part of God's plan. We may even want the old proverbial saying to play out in their life: *what goes around comes around*. As Christians, we are to follow the Lord Jesus' command to "love your enemies and pray for those who persecute you" (Matt 5:44), leaving the vengeance to God. But it's hard to let it go; we want to take matters into our own hands, because our sinful desire craves the opposite of what God wants.

The end of the story in Genesis is one with a profound and compelling tale and great application for us all today. One young man (Joseph) who was thrown into a well and then sold into slavery by his brothers is *now the one who can dictate the fate of his brothers*. The tables have turned—Joseph now has the earthly power to kill his brothers.

After Jacob's death, his brothers feared for their lives, and rightfully so. But the power of God's word in Gen 50:20 comes to life by his divine intervention in one man! "But as for you, you meant evil against me; but God meant it for good in order to bring it about as it is this day, to save many people alive."

There was something more powerful at work in Joseph than his earthly power. Joseph did the one thing that we should adhere to daily—let the influence of God's characteristics come to life for the good of all. Joseph allowed his supernatural God, in all his glorious attributes, come to fruition in his life.

One man could have killed his family, but he allowed the records to show that one person who had the power of God governing his life could make the difference in healing, saving, restoring, and renewing lives—all for the glory of God! And we individually can do the same when we allow Jesus Christ to be Lord of our life. *It only takes one who can make a difference—and it starts with you, today!*

> You intended to harm me, but God intended it all for good. He brought me to this position so I could save the lives of many people. (Gen 50:20)

Glossary

A

Abandoned (deserted, forsaken, cast aside, unused, *but in Christ you're never stranded!*)

Able (*capable and qualified for having the power, skill, and means to work for the Lord!*)

Abundance (large quantity, mass, *an extremely plentiful life as a believer in Jesus!*)

Acceptance (receive something suitable, approved, *welcoming his word in your life!*)

Access (a means of entering a place—*your entrance into heaven as a believer in Christ!*)

Accomplish (achieve, complete, fulfill, finish, concluded, *our victory in Jesus Christ!*)

Accountable (responsible, bound to obeying, liable, *we're to blame and will be held!*)

Accused (charged with a crime, charges against the guilty, *but in Christ you're innocent!*)

Acknowledge (*accept the truth of God's word, bow to it, and address it in your life!*)

Action (doing something, aim towards, *steps and efforts taken to know our Lord more!*)

Admit (*acknowledge, profess, and confess that Jesus Christ is Lord of your life!*)

Advantage (*once we surrender to Christ—there's new life in him, sins forgiven, transformed, power of his indwelling Spirit at work in us, faithful servants, eternal life!*)

Advice (*guidance, recommendation, direction, and pointers provided in God's word!*)

Affection (*a gentle fondness of love, endearment, friendship we can have with Christ!*)

Agape Love (the highest form of love, *the love of God for man, and of man for God!*)

Agreement (*in harmony, accordance with God's ways in your life!*)

Aim (*work towards, set one's sights on, pursue, strive for, target Christlikeness!*)

Alert (readiness for action, *discerning towards a threat or danger that could be harmful!*)

Align (*arrange your life in an order that positions and sets you toward Christlikeness!*)

Alliance (*a union for mutual benefit, a bonded association with Christ in your life!*)

Allows (approve of, pleased with, invest, entrust, *yield to, and acknowledge his ways!*)

Almighty (absolute overall and unlimited power in all things—*nothing compares to God!*)

Alone (having no one present in your life, singleness, *but in Christ he's always there!*)

Alternative (*available as another opportunity of relief, like accepting Christ as Savior!*)

Ambition (a strong desire to achieve something, intention, purpose, *a goal to serve God!*)

Anew (a new, different, and typically more positive way, *a fresh new beginning in him!*)

Anger (a strong feeling of hostility and rage, *but in Christ he can provide self-control!*)

Ambition (a strong desire to achieve something, *an intent to know and grow in Christ!*)

Anointed (chosen for a position and *once in Christ you're his candidate for service!*)

Anxiety (a reaction to a stressful situation, *but God's word provides us comfort!*)

Apart (separated away from, distant, far away, *cut off, let go for good—it's done!*)

Apostasy (the abandonment, betrayal defection and desertion of faith—*spiritual doom!*)

Apparent (clearly visible, understood, plain, striking, recognizable, *manifest Godliness!*)

Apply (make an effort, use, exercise, put into practice, *show commitment to his word!*)

Appointed (specified, determined, allotted, assigned, *designated, chosen for his glory!*)

Approval (to be real and true, having a positive and *favorable opinion of him in us!*)

Arrogance (attitude of superiority, *extreme sense of one's importance, spiritually weak!*)

Ashamed (embarrassed, guilty because of an action, *one choice for Christ removes it all!*)

Ask (*call for and seek for his counsel, beg and crave for his direction and guidance!*)

Assumption (accepted as true without proof, *God's word is precept upon precept!*)

Atonement (*restitution, satisfied a wrongdoing, reconciling with God through Jesus!*)

Attempt (do one's best, strive, *make every effort, and give one's all for the Lord!*)

Attention (*take notice, away, observe, regard as in paying attention to the Scripture!*)

Attitude (way of thinking, perspective, your approach, your feelings—*good or bad?*)

Authority (*the power of right to give orders in our life such as God's word in us!*)

Awe (*reverential respect, admiration, wonder, and amazement in all that God has done!*)

B

Balance (*stability, steadiness and footing in our daily life, such as God's word at work!*)

Barren (too poor to produce, unfruitful, *but in Christ fruitfulness can be abundant!*)

Barrier (an obstacle that prevents movement or access, a hurdle, *a spiritual roadblock*)

Basics (*the essential facts, principles, and realities of God's word active in us, daily!*)

Behavior (one's conduct, actions, practices, manners, ways, *habits—pure or impure?*)

Benefit (*an advantage or profit gained from, such as our eternal inheritance in Christ!*)

Bind (*tied, fastened together, shackled, and secured in Christ once we believe in him!*)

Bitterness (*anger and resentment that can be removed once a believer in Christ!*)

Blame (*one held accountable, condemnation, accused, but in Christ you're forgiven!*)

Blameless (innocent of wrongdoing, free from blame, *faultless in God's eyes as his!*)

Blasphemy (the unforgivable sin, ungodliness, disrespect, unholy, *but the Lord forgives!*)

Belief (an acceptance that a statement is true, *free from doubt in who you are in Christ!*)

Believer (one who believes *that something is effective, a follower and disciple of Christ!*)

Birth—Spiritual (*one who has been born into the family of God and craves a fellowship with other believers—and a desire to grow, develop and mature in Christlikeness!*)

Blessed (our inner state of well-being, *the full impact of God's presence in our lives!*)

Blessings (*God's favor and goodness, his goodwill and happiness in our lives!*)

Blindness (poor perception, *inability to see anything that is spiritually impure or hurtful!*)

Blood of Christ (*sacrificial death and full atoning work of Jesus on our behalf!*)

Boasting (excessively proud, self-satisfied about oneself—*no place in God's house!*)

Body of Christ (*collection and unity of true believers in a place serving, praising Christ!*)

Boldness (willingness—quality of a strong and clear appearance, *fearless for God!*)

Breath of life (the life and power of God, given to man to operate him, get him going, set him in motion, but the key lies in this—*who controls our on and off button?*)

Burdensome (difficult to carry out or fulfill, *only with God's help can we persevere!*)

Business of God (*the manage and stewardship of God's ways for his purpose and plan!*)

Busyness (a lot of things to do in life *that can lead to a disconnection from God!*)

C

Calamity (an event causing great distress, affliction, crisis, adversity, *temporary setback!*)

Calculating (scheming, ruthless behavior, self-interests, *driven by the flesh rather than the spirit!*)

Calling (a strong urge toward a particular way of life, mission, *course of action for God!*)

Callous (insensitive, cruel disregard for others, cold-hearted, heart of stone, *not of God!*)

Carelessness (failure to give *attention to God* in an area that could avoid harm or errors!)

Caring (*a kindhearted and genuine concern for all people in a Christlike fashion!*)

GLOSSARY

Chance (possibility of something happening, *an opportunity and hope to make it right!*)

Change (different, converted, transformed, *a Godly makeover for his glory!*)

Character (personality, attributes, *identity, qualities, the uniqueness of Christ in us!*)

Choice (select, decide, option, course of action, solution, *way out from the bad to good!*)

Chosen (*selected, fitting, suitable, called for, expected, preferred by God for his glory!*)

Christian (*one who believes in, professes, and follows all the ways of Jesus Christ!*)

Christianity (*belief in the teachings of Christ's life, death, and resurrection, good news!*)

Christlike (the result of Christian growth and maturity, *exemplifying behaviors of Christ!*)

Church (*the body—all those who have placed their faith in Jesus Christ for salvation!*)

Citizenship (*citizens of heaven on earth with our eternal resting place in his kingdom!*)

Clarity (clear, simplicity, plain, understandable—*no confusion, such as God's word!*)

Cleansing (intent to clean something thoroughly, purify, *Christ can wash away our sins!*)

Cling (*grasp, clench, grip, hold onto "tightly" all of God's ways for your life!*)

Comfort (a state of ease, freedom from pain, *a reassurance of God's peace in us!*)

Comfort Zone (behavioral state of anxiety control, *lack of spiritual growth!*)

Command (authoritative order, instruct, charge, *require, prescribed from God!*)

Commitment (*dedicated, devoted, faithful, attentive to a cause for our good—his glory!*)

Communication (*God communicates to us through his word and we to him in prayer!*)

Community (*a body who loves Jesus Christ and fellowships and supports each other!*)

GLOSSARY 147

Communion (*sharing of intimate thoughts, our remembrance of what Christ did for us!*)

Compare (contrast, differentiate—difference between, side by side, *flesh vs. spirit!*)

Compelled (forced, pressured or *an obligation to do something like living out his word!*)

Complacent (self-satisfied, proud, pleased with self, careless, lazy, *spiritually flawed!*)

Complainer (dissatisfaction, grumbler, moaner, whiner, finding fault, *spiritually toxic!*)

Completion (*the fulfillment, fruition and his successful work in us until Glory!*)

Compromise (agreement, settled, tradeoff, cooperate, give and take; *God or world?*)

Condemnation (very strong disapproval of, *but there is none who belong to Jesus Christ!*)

Confessions (admitting guilt, owning up, accountable, profess, expose, *a Godly act!*)

Confidence (belief we can rely on another, *a firm trust like our position with Christ!*)

Confirm (*establish correctness*, discover, determine, grasp, take in, *cling to his truths!*)

Conflict (a dispute that can lead to discord and division—*so often it's the work of Satan!*)

Conform (comply with rules, abide by, obey, agree to, fulfill, respect, *stick to God!*)

Confusion (*lack of understanding*, uncertainty, doubt, hesitancy, *enemy at work!*)

Connection (relationship, *linked together, relevant, relatable, bonded with the Lord!*)

Conscience (awareness, knowledge of right and wrong, *the key is applying God's word!*)

Consecrate (*as true believers our lives are a living sacrifice to him, separated from evil!*)

Consequences (*a result or effect of an action, outcome, end result could be bad!*)

Consistent (*done the same way over time, accurate, no variation from God's word!*)

Consuming (devour, take, feast on, engaging, deeply felt, *filling our minds with him!*)

Contentment (happiness, satisfaction, pleasure, comfort, *gratified with his provisions!*)

Contrary (opposite and inconsistent, *such as the ways of the world vs. God's ways!*)

Contrast (*strikingly different, as believers in Christ we're unlike anything of this world!*)

Conversation (a talk between people, *one that the Lord welcomes from us every day!*)

Conviction (declaring someone guilty, *a position that can be made right once in Christ!*)

Cooperate (work jointly towards the same result, *together with God every day!*)

Correction (making something right, rectifying, *all cleared up when we accept Christ!*

Corruption (dishonesty, deception, wrongdoing, *misconduct that's not a life in Christ!*)

Counsel (advice, guidance, direction, *enlightenment facts from his Spirit for our good!*)

Covenant (a binding agreement, *life-or-death agreement between two—you and God!*)

Creation (completeness, totality, fulfillment, or perfection—*God's awesomeness!*)

Creator (Someone Who brings something *into existence and sustains it- God at work!*)

Credibility (trustworthy, character, reliable, dependable, *reputation of a Godly person!*)

Cross (*the intersection of God's love and his justice, dead to self, following Christ!*)

Crown (*an honor received for our good and faithful works and a cause for great joy!*)

Crucial (critical in the success or failure of something, significant, *gamechanger!*)

Cunning (having skill in achieving one's end, deceptive, crafty, *scheming, not good!*)

D

Danger (possibility of suffering or harm, hazard, risk, *instability when not in Christ!*)

Darkness (partial or total absence of light, gloom, *dullness, void, and blackness!*)

Death (the end of physical life, *but as believers in Christ spiritual life continues forever!*)

Deceive (causing one to believe *what's not true, mislead, fool, cheat, double-crosser!*)

Decision (a resolution, settled, *once and for all when you accept Christ as Lord!*)

Declines (refuse to take advantage of, turn down, pass up, *could change your life!*)

Defiance (open resistance, bold disobedience, *disregard, rebellious—be careful!*)

Delight (*please someone greatly, what the Lord desires from us in our daily life!*)

Demand (insistent request, an order, ultimatum, urge, stipulation, *challenge to get right!*)

Demonstrate (show how something is done, display, illustrate, *exemplify his qualities*)

Depend (*controlled by, rely on, be based on, rest and lean on God for all things!*)

Depraved (corrupt, wicked, lead astray, poison another, defile, infect—*not of God!*)

Desires (want, yearning, longing, craving, an *eagerness, enthusiasm to know God more!*)

Despair (*complete loss or absence of hope*, unhappiness, discouragement, depression!)

Desperate (feeling a hopeless sense, at one's end, *but not in Christ for you are anew!*)

Destroy (put an end to, damage, tear down, break up, devastate, *enemy's goal!*)

Determined (made a firm decision, resolved, *not to change when you accept Christ!*)

Develop (form, grow, more mature, *flourish, blossom, succeed in all his ways!*)

Devise (think up, come up with, formulate, design, *work out a plan to know God more!*)

Devour (consume, gorge oneself, gobble up—*things we should do with God's word!*)

Difficult (need effort and skill to achieve, weary, tough, *without God's—it's impossible!*)

Diligence (persistent effort, attention to detail, continuance, *an intent to please him!*)

Disadvantage (*an unfavorable circumstance, a defect, a liability, could be costly!*)

Disagree (a different opinion, fail to agree, challenge, argue, quarrel, *be careful!*)

Discernment (*God-gifted ability to judge well, wise, sharp, insight, so needed today!*)

Discontent (dissatisfied, lack of contentment, a sense of grievance, *spiritually crippling!*)

Discourage (cause someone to lose confidence, enthusiasm, *not a Christ-like attribute!*)

Distract (prevent from giving full attention to something, disturb, confuse, *devils work!*)

Disobedience (fail or refuse to obey rules or authority, neglect, ignore, *enemies' goal!*)

Disposition (*spiritual—the way we respond to life and most importantly, God. Our response to him should be the most important thing in our minds, daily!*)

Divine (*Godly, Godlike, Saintly, Spiritual, Heavenly, Holy—God's ways!*)

Division (the act of separating, breaking up, splitting, severing, *disconnecting from the bad to good*)

Doer (*takes an active part, doesn't just think about it, "achieving God's directives"!*)

Doubt (connotes the idea of weakness in faith, negative attitude, or action—*not of God!*)

E

Effective (successful in producing a desired result, valuable, *such as our walk with God!*)

Effort (a vigorous or determined attempt, endeavor, an *all-out exertion to serve him!*)

Elevate (*raise and lift up that higher position you possess in Christ—every day!*)

Embrace (hold closely in one's arms, clasp to, enclose, *entwine oneself around the Lord!*)

Emotions (a natural state of mind, feeling, sensation, *reaction or response, passion for?*)

Emptiness (contain nothing, worthless, ineffective, *once wholly in Christ—you're filled!*)

Encourage (*supporter, confidence or hope to one, uplift, helpful, a Christlike enforcer!*)

Endurance (tolerate, bear, patience, acceptance, persistence, *a staying power in him!*)

Engage (become involved, participate in, embark on, *play a key role in all his ways!*)

Enhance (*intensify, increase, further improve the quality of your walk with the Lord!*)

Enlightenment (learning, development, insight, *advancement in all of God's ways!*)

Enthusiasm (intense and eager enjoyment *nothing like a relationship with Jesus Christ!*)

Envy (jealousy, covet, bitterness, resentment, a wrong desire, *a sinful vice that cripples!*)

Equality (state of being equal, *fairness, impartial, we're all created by God equally!*)

Error (a mistake, oversight, misinterpretation, *a misconception, but God can fix!*)

Establish (set up, start, begin, get going, *bring into being your intended life for him!*)

Everlasting (forever, without end, imperishable, immortal, deathless—*priceless!*)

Evidence (proof which confirms, reveals, displays manifests, *signifies your identity in Christ!*)

Evil (wicked, bad, corrupt, immoral, sin, black-hearted—*life or death matter!*)

Exalt (hold someone in high regard, *glorify, praise, worship, reverence to the Holy One!*)

Example (*characteristic of its kind, illustrating one's case, a representative for Christ!*)

Excitement (*feeling of great enthusiasm and eagerness as you grow closer to the Lord!*)

Exclusive (complete, full, whole, absolute, *your undivided attention to the Lord!*)

Excuse (seek to justify, rationalize, overlook, disregard, *turn a deaf ear to good news!*)

Expectation (belief something will happen, anticipation, *future outlook for our good!*)

Experience (practical contact, acquaintance, exposure to, *understanding of him in you!*)

F

Failure (lack of success, non-fulfilling, *but as a true child of God you have not failed!*)

Faith (complete trust, confidence, hopefulness, belief, *dependence upon his word!*)

Faithfulness (unfailing loyalty to someone, *consistently putting into practice his ways!*)

Faithless (disloyal, unfaithful, unreliable, *even though we're faithless, God's faithful!*)

Fatalism (belief that all events are inevitable, *out of God's control, it debilitates faith!*)

Favor (gaining approval, acceptance, pleasure or *special benefits or blessings from him!*)

Fear (terror, alarmed, anxious, worry, uneasy, distress, doubt, dread, *spiritual weakness!*)

Feel (awareness, sense, discern, *conscious of something powerful at work in us!*)

Find (discover, realize, become aware; appears, shows, and *manifest his word in us*)

Fixated (*obsessed with, gripped by, devoted to, focused—as we should be as Christians!*)

Flee (run away from danger, escape, leave, get away quickly, *spiritually discerning!*)

Flesh (*the part of a believer that disagrees with the Spirit—they cannot coexist!*)

Filth (foul, disgusting dirt, contamination, and garbage—*that's not a spiritual virtue!*)

Focus (*center of interest, focal point, backbone, anchor, basis of the Controlling One!*)

Follower (*a devoted person to a cause, companion, admirer, supporter, lover of Christ!*)

Fool (acting unwisely, imprudent, idiot, *a halfwit not taking God's word seriously!*)

Foothold (*an issue of who influences the heart. Is it the Lord or the enemy? A place where you can put your foot safely and securely when climbing- like the Rock!*)

Footstool (is a symbol of lowliness, humility, and unimportance—*selflessness!*)

Forgetfulness (lose remembrance of, forget facts, *God's word is a fresh reminder daily!*)

Forgiveness (absolute forgiving, cleared, pardon, *God's mercy on us as sinners!*)

Foundation (starting point, heart, principle, fundamentals, cornerstone, *Godly position!*)

Freedom (*the power, right and privilege we have to speak of the good news of Christ!*)

Fruit of the Spirit (*Holy Spirit's presence, working in lives of true maturing believers!*)

Fruitfulness (*being useful for the work of the Lord in our daily lives for his Glory!*)

Fulfill (bring to completion, succeed, *bring about his good fruit in your daily life!*)

Futile (incapable of producing useful results, pointless, *but his Spirit in us can produce!*)

G

Genealogy (historic facts in Bible, importance of family to God, proof of prophecies)

Generosity (*the Christlike quality of genuine kindness, honorable, lack of any prejudice!*)

Gentleness (*supreme kindness, mild-mannered, tender, softness, courteous, considerate!*)

Genuine (someone who is authentic, real, legit, sound, sterling, *rightful in all his ways!*)

Gifts (given willingly, a present, offering, favor, inheritance, *bestowal from him to us!*)

GLOSSARY

Giving (handing over freely, *God's children providing others what he's gifted us with!*)

Glorify (praise, exalt, worship, reverence, adore, honor, bless, *magnify him in all we do!*)

Glory (*splendor, holiness and majesty of God, place of unfathomable praise and honor!*)

Goal (a future desired result to achieve something *as citizens of heaven on Earth!*)

God (*All Supreme Being, Creator, Who is Perfect in Power, Wisdom, and Goodness!*)

Godly Fear (*a reverent feeling to God, a deterrent to sin, and brings us closer to God!*)

God's Fairness (*living under God's righteous and just love, grace, and mercy!*)

God's Kingdom (the rule of an eternal, sovereign God over all the universe!)

God's Laws (his unchangeable divine nature, expression of love, joy, holy, just, good!)

God's Nature (*All Supreme—Holy, Just, Righteous, All-Omni, Loving Kind Creator!*)

God's Presence (*always present in believers by his Spirit; a strong relationship!*)

God's Promises (*to help strengthen our faith* and have something to hold on to!)

God's Protection (*heaven is our home—we are spiritually safe as believers in Christ!*)

God's Season (*appointed time for all seasons of life—part of living out God's plan!*)

God's Timing (*when all falls comfortably, naturally into place—in his appointed time!*)

God's View (*God always sees how all things work together to conform us to his image!*)

God's Will (*things that are in line with God's superior and supreme plan and purpose!*)

God's Word (the infallible *truth, righteous and goodness of all God's holy ways!*)

God's Work (*where we're equipped with his gift to benefit others and accomplish his good works in love and faithfulness—with his guidance—representing him!*)

Godliness (*the practice, exercise, and discipline of devoutness to God's word!*)

Good (quality, satisfactory, acceptable, high quality and standard, *up to his mark!*)

Goodness (*godly virtue, with integrity, honesty, truthful, honorable, righteous, caring!*)

Gossiper (betrayal of confidence, a perverse person stirring up dissension *not Godly!*)

Grace (*God's favor towards the unworthy, his goodwill, generosity, loving kindness!*)

Gratitude (*the godly quality of thankfulness, appreciation, recognition, credit, respect!*)

Greed (a strong selfish desire for something, most often worldly things—*and not God!*)

Growth (*the increasing, maturing, thriving, and sprouting of Christlikeness in us!*)

Guide ("*One*" *who shows the way to others, advice aimed at resolving life's problems!*)

Guilt (committed a crime, wrongdoing, *but cleared when accepting Christ as Savior!*)

H

Habits (a regular practice or custom that's hard to give up, *may be a spiritual detriment!*)

Half-heartedness (no enthusiasm or energy, *not "all in"—wholeheartedly for the Lord!*)

Happiness (feeling of joy, satisfaction, *one we should experience as Christians!*)

GLOSSARY

Hardheartedness (incapable of being moved to pity or tenderness, *no Christlike value!*)

Harmony (in tune simultaneously, sounds *joined together into whole units-as one!*)

Harvest (*spiritual users of our gifts in God's field to reap what we sow, sign of growth!*)

Hatred (intense dislike or ill will, *a poison that can destroy our spirit from within!*)

Healing (the process of becoming sound or healthy—*spiritually eased and relieved!*)

Health (*a continual spiritual treatment and nourishment of our heart, mind, and soul!*)

Heaven (physical reality beyond earth—*the spiritual reality where God lives, we can also!*)

Heavenly Father (first person of the Trinity—*Supreme Being, Creator, and Sustainer!*)

Hear (get, listen to, *discern, be informed*, told, made aware of, *given to understand him!*)

Heart (*the main part and core of our spiritual makeup in thoughts, actions, and words!*)

Heart-Set (*modeling the force of what's controlling the heart to the outside world! It's either glorifying God or not!*)

Heed (pay attention to take notice of, consider, *give ear to observe and apply his ways!*)

Hell (the total, conscious, eternal separation from God's blessings, *so choose Christ!*)

Helper (one that helps, aids, or assists *a Christlike assistant out of real love!*)

Holy Spirit (third person of the Trinity, Comforter, Counselor—*God in action in our life!*)

Honesty (*moral correctness, high principles, right mindedness, worthiness, Godly truth!*)

Honor (high respect, esteem, distinction, privilege, respect, *notable to the True God!*)

Hope (feeling of expectation for a certain thing to happen, *longing for a great outcome!*)

Hopelessness (absolute despair, no hope, feeling of lostness, *but in Christ hope's alive!*)

Hospitality (the *Christlike quality* of friendly and *generous reception of all people!*)

Humility (*Christlike modesty, a low view of oneself, lack of pride, godly meekness!*)

I

Idolatry (*worship of idols other than God, ungodliness and unholy in the eyes of God!*)

Ignore (refuse to notice, *disregard, leave out, disobey, defy!*)

Image (a representation of the external form, likeness, resemblance, portrayal—*godly!*)

Imitator (one who copies the behavior of another, a person *in high esteem—Jesus Christ!*)

Immaturity (not growing, *a "spiritual infant" looks and acts like a human infant!*)

Immoral (not conforming or accepting standards of morality, *spiritual lostness!*)

Immortal (*living forever, never dying or decaying for those who are in Jesus Christ!*)

Impact (a strong effect on others, highly influential, *make an impression for his glory!*)

Impartial (treatment of everyone fair and equal, *leave all doors open like God does!*)

Impatience (no patience, irritable, restless, *complete opposite of the fruit of the Spirit!*)

Imperative (necessary, mandatory, pressing, urgent, *could be dire—if not a Believer!*)

Important (great significant value, an effect on success, *like living out God's word daily!*)

Impression (a feeling or opinion about someone, view, perception, *image of him in us!*)

Impulsive (done without forethought, in many if not all cases, *no spiritual discernment!*)

Inclusive (*all around, all embracing and all in for the Lord -without hesitation!*)

Indifference (lack of concern, interest or sympathy, no feelings, *distant from godliness!*)

Influencer (*the power and impact we have on others when God's word is thriving in us!*)

Initiative (*ambition, motivation, and drive to assess God's word and move forward!*)

Insecure (unstable, weak, *not firmly fixed or grounded in the blanket of God's security!*)

Insensitive (showing no feelings for others, callous, *lacking God's guidance!*)

Instructions (order, command, directive, requirement, *stipulations given in his word!*)

Integrity (*Christlike quality of moral uprightness, high principles in line with God!*)

Interests (wanting to learn more about something, attentive, *real students of God's word!*)

Intentional (done on purpose, deliberate, thought out, *knowingly pleasing him, daily!*)

Interpret (explain the meaning of, *make clear, understand, resolve for our good purpose!*)

J

Jealousy (discontent, resentment, *it means we're not happy with what God's given us!*)

Jesus Christ (*God incarnate, second person of the Trinity, Lord, Redeemer, Messiah, King, Savior, Son of the Living God, Creator, Wonderful Counsellor, Righteous One, Bread of Life, Advocate, Lamb of God, Good Shepherd, Bridegroom, Son of Man, Alpha and Omega, The Way, Truth, and Life!*)

Joined (fixed together, connected, attached, *yoked, chained, locked in with him!*)

Journey (the act of moving, *making one's way down God's path of righteousness!*)

Joy (*greatest of pleasures*, happiness, delight, *rejoice and exultation of our life in Christ!*)

Judgement, Final (*unbelievers judged for their sins and cast into eternal separation!*)

Judging (*determine the biblical act of righteous and unrighteous behavior in a believer!*)

Justified (*declared righteous because of our faith in what Christ did for us on the cross!*)

K

Kindness (*generous concern for all, expecting nothing in return, true godly sincerity!*)

Knowing (realize, aware, understand, sense, recognize, *notice right from wrong!*)

Knowledge (comprehend, mastered, accomplishment, intelligence, *God's insight!*)

L

Learner (one who is learning a subject or skill, *how to utilize God's word in their life!*)

Led (*to be prompted, instructed, and directed by the Holy Spirit—he's leading our way!*)

Legalism (set of laws above the gospel, emphasizing a system of rules and regulations for achieving both salvation and spiritual growth, *opposite of God's grace!*)

Lessons (period of teaching, tutoring of the *Holy Spirit in accordance with God's word!*)

Life (Living Intentionally For Eternity, *the culmination of our real life in Christ!*)

Lifestyle (the way one lives, an *influenced behavior by either the flesh or Spirit!*)

Light (*the natural agent that stimulates light, brightness, the ray of Christ's light in us!*)

Lineage (ancestry, family, heritage, roots, background, bloodline, *succession!*)

Listener (*an attentive, intentional person who listens, hears, and applies God's word!*)

Living Out (*the strength of Christ's Spirit at work within us that's illuminating his joy!*)

Love (undeniable longing affection and *all-consuming passion of commitment to Christ!*)

Lustful (overwhelming sinful desire, pleasing oneself, *no regard for consequences!*)

Lying (untruthful, false, dishonest, deceptive, underhand, hollow-hearted, *spiritually ill!*)

M

Magnify (*make something appear larger, maximize, amplify, enhance his glory in you!*)

Malicious (someone in spite intending to do harm, *this is evil intent—and not Christlike!*)

Manage (*in charge of, control, take forward and handle God's word in your daily life!*)

Manipulate (control or influence a person unfairly, no scruples, *malicious maneuvering!*)

Materialism (a kind of worldliness where *God is gradually pushed off into a small corner*, and where *physical substance is more important than the spiritual matter!*)

Maturity (developed, effective and fruitful, *changed from pleasing self to pleasing God!*)

Mindset (an established set of attitudes that are *fixed and growing based on what's going into the mind—could be the spiritual gamechanger in our daily life!*)

Mortal (a human being subject to death, *but if in Christ as their Savior they're immortal!*)

Mercy (pity, compassion, kindness, forgiveness, *withholding punishment deserved!*)

Mirror (*spiritual—the transformed image of our new life and look as Christians!*)

Misled (*deceived by someone and being led in the wrong direction, lack of wisdom!*)

Motives (reason for doing something, not hidden, intention, motivation, *godly purpose!*)

Mourning (expression of deep sorrow for someone's death, grieve for, wail, *temporary!*)

N

Need (require something of necessity, essential, *very important in our life, like Christ!*)

Negative (no optimism, not desirable, pessimistic, bleak, harmful, *a spiritual detriment!*)

Neglect (fail to care of properly, untended, abandoned, *forsake his righteous ways!*)

Nurture (*care for—encourage the growth and development on the feeding of his word!*)

O

Obedience (comply with an order, respectful, duty, discipline, *conform to all his ways!*)

Obligation (legally bound to perform, duty, responsibility, *requirement to serve him!*)

Offering (put forward—*submit a gift to Christ. Our advancement to him for his glory!*)

Omnipotent (*unlimited power, able to do anything, Supreme, Most High, invincible!*)

Omnipresent (*present everywhere, infinite, boundless, immeasurable!*)

Omniscient (*all-knowing, all-wise, and all-seeing!*)

Opinion (a viewpoint or judgement formed about something, *line it up with God's word!*)

Opportunity (*chance, good time, occasion, moment, opening, option, go and seize-now!*)

Opposition (one that opposes, combats, fights against, and antagonizes another for their belief in a cause, *such as the enemy and unbelieving world against Christians!*)

Oppression (heavily weighed down in spirit, mind, or body, *but Jesus can set us free!*)

Overcome (prevail, get the better of, beat, tame, subdue, *get over, solve, triumph over!*)

P

Past (gone by in time and no longer existing—*such as your sins when you accept Christ!*)

Patience (*restraint, calm, tolerance, even temperedness, composed, kindness, tranquil*)

Peace (restful, free from disturbance, stillness, solitude, *lack of interruptions-rest in him*)

Perception (ability to hear, see or be aware of something, *a notion of God's word*)

Perish (suffer death, expire, fall, *go the way of all flesh, be lost, eternal death!*)

Persecution (hostility, ill-treatment, *unfair and cruelty over a long period of time!*)

Perseverance (determination, diligence, patience, resolve, steadfast, *commitment to him!*)

Perspective (view, outlook, position, interpretation, frame of mind, approach—*God's lens!*)

Perpetual (neverending, long-lasting, without end, as *believers—permanently in Christ!*)

Planning (*decide, arrange, organize, work out, and expect God's word to develop you!*)

Pleasing (feel happy, satisfied, pleasant, acceptable, enjoyable, *delightful in him!*)

Pleasures (happiness, satisfaction, delight, gladness, contentment, *enjoy his provisions!*)

Position (*your location, place, spot, and orientation in life directed by God!*)

Potential (*showing the capacity to develop into something, a life in the making for God!*)

Precept (*a principle, doctrine intended to regulate our behavior, such as God's word!*)

Predestined (*the biblical doctrine that God in all his sovereignty chooses certain individuals to be saved, but the choice to accept him is "always available for anyone"!*)

Preparation (devise, put together, get ready, train, educate, discipline, *godly grooming!*)

Priority (regarded or treated as more important, first concern, *greatest importance—God!*)

Position (a situation, orientation, posture, attitude, *your place grounded in him!*)

Positive (optimism, confidence; *helpful, beneficial, cheerful, godly encourager!*)

Possession (*the ownership and control of God in us, proclaiming his excellencies!*)

Power (*is an inherent characteristic of God, the Christian life is an empowerment from God, the same power that raised Christ from the dead indwells in believers today!*)

Praise (*wholehearted expression of approval, admiration, and commendation to Christ!*)

GLOSSARY

Prayer (a precious avenue that God has provided where we can raise our hearts by talking to him, communicating *all our thoughts, needs, and desires—it's an intentional act!*)

Prepare (*get into spiritual shape, equip oneself with the Armor of God and put in action!*)

Pressures (unavoidable part of life on earth, a squeezing and crushing; it's the application of any power, but as believers in Jesus Christ, he gives us relief from these forces!)

Pride (a sinful, arrogant, haughty, self-reliant attitude or spirit that causes a person to have an inflated or puffed-up view of themselves; *kingdom killer!*)

Priority (*something deeply important to us that we care about, like our time in his word!*)

Procrastinate (*put off, delay; undecided, to take one's time, hesitate; spiritually lazy!*)

Produce (make, build, put together, assemble, process, *mass-produce for his glory!*)

Progress (*moving forward, advancing, and making headway in our daily Christian life!*)

Promise (one declaring they will do exactly what they say, *such as God's plans for our salvation and blessings to his people!*)

Propitiation (appeasing wrath of sinners-*reconciled to God because of Christ's sacrifice!*)

Provide (make available for use, supply, assign, present, *he bestowed for our use!*)

Pruning (*cut away things in our spiritual life that are not productive and hinder growth!*)

Purging (*to purify and separate us from things that are impure in our lives!*)

Purify (cleanse, refine, freshen; *strained of contaminants, sifted, and made pure by God!*)

Purpose (reason why something is done, *a Christlike desire to achieve a good outcome!*)

Pursue (follow someone, go after, run after, chase, *proceed along his path constantly!*)

Q

Quality (the degree of excellence, standard, condition, character, worth, *godly values!*)

R

React (behave in a particular way, retaliate, oppose, revolt against, *conduct oneself!*)

Reality (*real world, the godly truth of his existence at work in our real life!*)

Rebellion (*an act of violent resistance, civil disobedience, disorder, unrest, anarchy!*)

Receptive (willing to consider, accept, *the quality of receiving the truth of his word!*)

Recognize (*identify, acknowledge an area of concern, and gain support from the Lord!*)

Redemption (*act of being saved from sin, God paid it all through his Son-Jesus Christ!*)

Reformed (*changed from worse to better—when we allow his Spirit to work in us!*)

Refuge (a condition of being safe or sheltered from pursuit, haven; *he's our security!*)

Refuse (one that is not willing to do something, rejected as worthless; *spiritual defeat!*)

Rejection (refuse something that could be of benefit, *a danger to deny the truth of God!*)

Rejoice (*feeling of unbelievable joy, transporting that delight back to the ears of God!*)

Relationship (*connection, bond, relevance, association; to be a part of God's family!*)

Religion (*belief and worship of the One True God, real godliness in practice, performing all duties to God and our fellow believers, in obedience to his divine command!*)

GLOSSARY

Remembrance (the act of reminding ourselves all that God has done for us in Christ!)

Remove (cut off, detach, *separate ourselves away from anything that's not Christlike!*)

Renewed (*a new person, restored life, spiritually new, a new creation in Christ as Lord!*)

Repent (*change one's mind and attitude, purpose from a course of bad conduct to God!*)

Repetition (*repeating something, copying, quoting God's word in our daily life!*)

Representative (*characteristic illustrative, an exemplary of Christlikeness in our life!*)

Reproach (*find unacceptable, object to, dislike, be against, such as false teachings!*)

Reprobate (an evildoer, wretched person, good for nothing, *and not acceptable to God!*)

Reputation (belief held about someone, overall quality recognized by others, *is it Christ?*)

Resolve (settle, find a solution to a problem, *sort out, clarify, set right in his sight!*)

Response (something said or done as a reaction to something—*a productive answer!*)

Responsibility (*godly duty to deal with something who needs to be made right-lovingly!*)

Rest (*a refreshed and recharged spirit when grounded and dependent upon the Lord!*)

Results (the outcome, findings, effects, *the byproducts of his fruits at work in our life!*)

Resurrection (*a rising again; a return from death to life; as the resurrection of Christ, its strength for today—and a bright hope for tomorrow!*)

Reunion (*a reuniting after separation, our glorious reconnection with fellow believers!*)

Reverence (*high esteem, deep respect, our favor, worship, honor, and praise to God!*)

Rewards (*our Lord recompensing us out of his kindness a return for services well done!*)

Righteousness (morally correct, highest honor, justifiable, rightness, *acceptable—Christ!*)

Role (*our part and character on this earth that should be displaying Christ-like qualities!*)

S

Safeguard (a measure taken to protect someone, a provision, *our buffer is Jesus Christ!*)

Salvation (*being delivered, by God's grace, from sin and its consequence of eternal punishment and being raised to newness of life in Christ Jesus!*)

Saved (*rescued and delivered* from the hands of the enemy and eternal death!)

Sanctified (*to be set apart from the world and used for God's holy work!*)

Satan (accuser, destroyer, prince of evil spirits, *the adversary of God and Christ!*)

Satisfied (to meet the expectations, needs, or desires of; pleased, *content with all of God!*)

Sealed (*to guarantee security and indicate our authentic ownership of God in us!*)

Seek (an attempt to find something, pursue it, or chase after it, *a relentless quest for God!*)

Self-Control (*ability to control self, in emotions, desires, words and deed, a godly fruit!*)

Selflessness (*more concerned with the needs and well-being of others than themselves!*)

Selfishness (the excessive concern of oneself, *their own advantage and pleasure!*)

Sensitivity (*aware of the needs and emotions of others, responds with Christlikeness!*)

Sensuality (*enjoyment or pursuit of physical pleasure, a carnal passion of ungodliness!*)

GLOSSARY

Servant (one who performs duties for others, *a selfless helper in all facets!*)

Service (action of helping someone, *true Christlike kindness—keep in good condition!*)

Shameful (causing disgrace, embarrassing, dishonorable, *Christ can remove all shame!*)

Sharing (have a portion with another, participate, *our Christlike fellowship with others!*)

Shrewd (clever, *calculating*, sharp-witted, canny, wise; *it's another enemy's mask!*)

Sight (ability to see, visual perception, observe, *make out the truth!*)

Significant (*sufficiently of great importance, worthy of, notable, like Christ in us!*)

Sin (wicked, morally wrong, fallen, unholy, tainted, impure, *failure to do what is right*)

Slander (a false statement damaging to a person, it's malicious lying and *God hates it!*)

Slave *Spiritual* (the "possession" of his master, in obedience to his commands, *their actions signify ownership—the flesh or the Spirit!*)

Slow (*designed to do so in an unhurried manner, deliberate, unrushed, relaxed, comfortable, steady, and easy, a gentle approach, in many cases spiritually driven!*)

Sly (conniving, scheming, deceitful, *manipulative, sneaky, an enemy masquerade!*)

Solidity (the quality of being firm or strong in structure, *your steadfastness in Christ!*)

Sovereignty (*supreme authority, power, dominion, and control!*)

Speech (the ability to express inner thoughts; *it's the utterance of good or bad things!*)

Spiritual (*living out God's presence in our life—in a way that glorifies him!*)

Spiritual *Leader* (*a servant who influences people to think, say, and behave in ways that enhance their spiritual life to areas of discipleship and service for the Lord!*)

Standards (quality levels, excellence, guidelines, benchmarks, *God's requirements!*)

Steadfastness (*one's firm and unwavering faith in the Lord so nothing can deter!*)

Steps (act of movement, in stride; course of action, strategy; *an initiative to follow God!*)

Steward (*a man's relationship to God, identifies God as owner—and man as manager!*)

Storm (*a rushing, raging, or violent agitation used to mature, strengthen Christlikeness!*)

Strategy (approach designed to achieve an overall aim, *a grand design of Christlikeness!*)

Strengthen (to become stronger, to add, *increase an obligation or authority!*)

Stronghold (*see foothold!*)

Stubborn (unwilling to change attitude or position, *inflexible, bull-headed, pigheaded!*)

Stumbling Block (thing or person *who keeps another from a relationship with God!*)

Submission (*obedient to an authority and the very act of submitting to them for control!*)

Success (the outcome of an aim or purpose, *a victory when we yield to God's guidance!*)

Suffering (hardship, distress, tribulation, pain, agony, sadness, *not for long as believers!*)

Surrender (*choose to give up the fight between self and God and surrender to his will!*)

T

Talents (*gifts from God in the form of a person's calling or natural ability—glorify Him!*)

Task (work *to be done, duty, responsibility, and charge-such as the Great Commission!*)

GLOSSARY

Teaching (*is one of the gifts of the Holy Spirit, the ability to explain God's word clearly, to instruct and communicate knowledge, as it relates to the faith and truths of the Bible!*)

Temptation (the desire or urge to do something *wrong or unwise!*)

Tension (stress, anxiety, nervousness, agitation, pressure, *restlessness, uncertainty*)

Test (*challenging situation that prompts us to discern how God would have us respond!*)

Thankfulness (*should be a way of life, naturally flowing from our hearts and mouths ongoing every day—because God is worthy!*)

Thoughts (*an idea produced by thinking of an image; it can be good or bad, depending on what we're feeding into our minds that can produce something pure or impure!*)

Time (an allotted or used moment that *can yield a negative or positive experience!*)

Tithing (*a joyful, voluntary giver who trusts God* as the source of all he's given them to supply their needs—*they're a cheerful giver, giving back portions of God's blessings!*)

Together (in alliance, bonded as one, cooperate, partners, *in one accord with God!*)

Tolerance (allow and accept an occurrence or practice, *ensure it lines up with Scripture!*)

Tongue (*spiritual—it's either honoring the Lord or spewing venom that God forbids!*)

Transformed (changed, altered, reshaped, renewed, remade, *and made to be used!*)

Transparent (see-through, uncloudy, clearly exposed, *real Christlikeness seen in you!*)

Trial (a cause of great suffering, *cross to bear, but God will give us strength!*)

Trust (*a bold, confident, sure security, it's what we do because of the faith we're given, godly trust will not waiver because it is based on faith in the promises of God!*)

Truth (the quality of our *factual, genuine, authentic, and valid position in Christ!*)

Turn Away (move or face a different location, *your shift from ungodliness to godliness!*)

U

Unbeliever (person who has rejected Jesus Christ, and wants nothing to do with him, but he does want to have something to do with you, because he cares!)

Unchanging (*someone not changing, staying the same, caught in the enemy's trap!*)

Understanding (*perceive the intended and accurate meaning of God's word so you can live a true intentional life for God, today!*)

Unforgiveness (a *strong willingness* to restore what's broken, like taking poison and expecting someone else to die, *a spiritual killer; he forgave—so we can forgive!*)

Unholy (ungodly, godless, depraved, sinful, wicked *with no room in God's kingdom!*)

United (joined together for *a common purpose or common feeling with the Lord, daily!*)

Unity (joined as a whole, unified, *a oneness with God, identity, self-sameness!*)

Unrest (*that state of dissatisfaction, agitation, and being disturbed when the Lord is not present!*)

Urgent (immediate action, desperate, *a serious cry for God's help in a dire situation!*)

Usefulness (*serviceable, quality of having utilities [gifts] for use that bring value to God!*)

Utilize (*make practical and effective use of, deploy, bring into action for God!*)

V

Valid (well-founded, sound, defendable, strong, reliable, *convincingly Christlike!*)

Value (*level of something deserved, importance, worth, like our daily steps with God!*)

Verify (*make sure, demonstrate, justify, authenticate, confirm, substantiate him in us!*)

Victory (*that place in our relationship with God because he gives us the advantage or power over spiritual enemies, temptations, or in any struggle in life. In Christ we have the ultimate victory and the power of his indwelling Spirit alive and at work in us, daily!*)

Violence (force intended to hurt, damage, or kill; cruel, brutal, *no spiritual control!*)

Vital (necessary, essential, key, needed, *highest priority, such as his word alive in us!*)

W

Wait (*to stay for; rest or remain still in expectation of; wait for orders; the power of undeniable willingness and patience in his strength to get you to the next phase!*)

Walking (*moving at a regular pace, accompanying, guiding, moving in stride with him daily!*)

Want (a desire to possess, care for, crave, thirst for; desperate, *a yearning for Christ!*)

Warning (*Caution against danger, faults, or evil practices that can lead us astray!*)

Weakness (*means we don't have what it takes, and we desperately need God daily!*)

Weariness (*the weights of the world and exhaustions of everyday life lead us to this overly debilitating state, so we need God as our focal point to help balance this life!*)

Wealth (*spiritual—God's intelligence and wisdom in our life, also his knowledge of truth and good, but true wealth is to have eternal life in Christ!*)

Wholly (*entirely all in without any reservation, and to the maximum extent for the Lord!*)

Willing (ready, eager, prepared, intend, desire, order, command, *a want of him in you!*)

Wisdom (*having experience, wise, knowledgeable, discerning, Godly judgement!*)

Witness (*someone who boldly and with confidence conveys to the world the evidence of what Jesus Christ did to transform their life into a faithful and serving believer!*)

Worship (*that feeling of complete reverence and adoration for our Lord and King!*)

Worry (*spiritual defeater that accomplishes nothing; Christians, don't worry, trust God!*)

Worthy (*deserving merits, excellence in qualities, an important person like Christ!*)

Y

Yearning (an intense longing for something, craving, hunger, *eagerness of him—now!*)

Yielding (submissive, inclined to give in, compliant, *a person who is bendable to God!*)

Yoke (*the weight of a task, or obligation; if joined with the right and most effective partner it goes in a direction that will yield a very productive Christlike result!*)

Z

Zeal (great energy, enthusiasm, love, devotedness, appetite, vigor, *a strong and undeniable passion for him in my life today!*)

Bibliography

"Are Many Practices and Traditions in Christianity Actually Pagan in Origin?" https://www.gotquestions.org/pagan-Christianity.html.

Clark, Heather. "2020 'State of the Bible' Report Finds Few Americans Read Bible Daily." *Christian News*, July 24, 2020. https://christiannews.net/2020/07/24/2020-state-of-the-bible-report-finds-few-americans-read-bible-daily/.

"How Can I Learn to Trust that God Is in Control?" https://www.gotquestions.org/God-is-in-control.html.

McLean, Liz. "Leave Your Rank at the Door When You Choose Your Next Career." *Task & Purpose* (blog), March 27, 2015. https://taskandpurpose.com/military-life/your-rank-does-not-define-what-your-next-career-should-be/.

Roat, Alyssa. "7 Facts You Didn't Know about Nimrod in the Bible." *Crosswalk* (blog), December 15, 2020. https://www.crosswalk.com/faith/bible-study/facts-about-nimrod-in-the-bible.html.

Scott, Walter. "Marmion: A Tale of Flodden." https://www.enotes.com/topics/marmion/quotes/oh-what-tangled-web-we-weave-when-first-we.

Sermon Notes by Dr. Tony Evans. "Tony Evans Sermons | Mar 04, 2019. Maturity: The Goal of Spiritual Growth." *YouTube*, March 4, 2019. https://www.youtube.com/watch?v=ONlQ8QrFXMY

Spurgeon, Charles. "The Power of Prayer and the Pleasure of Praise." https://www.spurgeon.org/resource-library/sermons/the-power-of-prayer-and-the-pleasure-of-praise.

———. "Spurgeon's Verse Expositions of the Bible." https://www.truthaccordingtoscripture.com/commentaries/spe/genesis-22.php#.Y1Gk9dfMK5c.

"What Are the Consequences of Sin?" https://www.gotquestions.org/consequences-of-sin.html.

"What Is Circumcision of the Heart?" https://www.gotquestions.org/circumcision-of-the-heart.html.

"Why Americans Go (and Don't Go) to Religious Services." August 1, 2018. https://www.pewresearch.org/religion/2018/08/01/why-americans-go-to-religious-services/.